Information Security
Cost Management

Information Security Cost Management

Ioana V. Bazavan · Ian Lim

CRC Press
Taylor & Francis Group
Boca Raton London New York

CRC Press is an imprint of the
Taylor & Francis Group, an **informa** business

CRC Press
Taylor & Francis Group
6000 Broken Sound Parkway NW, Suite 300
Boca Raton, FL 33487-2742

First issued in paperback 2019

ISBN-13: 978-0-8493-9275-7 (hbk)
ISBN-13: 978-0-367-39042-6 (pbk)

Visit the Taylor & Francis Web site at
http://www.taylorandfrancis.com

and the CRC Press Web site at
http://www.crcpress.com

Acknowledgments

I would like to thank my parents and my closest friends for their undying support of this endeavor. It was a mad dash at the end and I could not have gotten through it without their encouragement and praise. Thanks also to Ian for coming up with the idea for this book and proposing it to me; it was great being a team again.

Ioana

I owe my deepest gratitude to my mother, who raised our family singlehandedly and showed us how to live with fortitude, compassion, and contentment through the difficult times. I would also like to thank my wife for her constancy and support throughout the writing of this book. Thank you, Ioana; I could not have run this race alone. I would be remiss not to mention the family and friends who encouraged me, pushed me, and kept me on the path until I finished the book. Most importantly, I would like to dedicate this book to the memory of my uncle, who passed away this year. The legacy of your lightheartedness and generosity lives on in the hearts of those who love you.

Ian

The Authors

Ioana V. Bazavan, CISSP, is manager of Information Security Access Services at Safeway, Inc. She manages a team of 18 people charged with providing systems access to Safeway's users and applications. She has been heavily involved in the design and implementation of Safeway's identity management strategy and technologies.

Previously, Ms. Bazavan was a manager in Accenture's global security practice, specializing in holistic security solutions that focused on users and organizations, as well as on systems. She gained extensive experience in security policy, standard and process design and implementation, compliance solutions based on industry and regulatory standards, security strategy and organization design, user training and awareness, incident response, risk assessment, user management systems, infrastructure security, and systems development methodology.

Ms. Bazavan has industry experience in financial services, government, high tech, resources, and retail. She is published, along with Ian Lim, in the fifth edition of Auerbach's *Information Security Management Handbook*, edited by Tipton and Krause. Ms. Bazavan has also been interviewed for radio broadcasts and print and Internet articles on security. She has been invited to speak at conferences such as RSA and is a frequent guest lecturer for the MBA program at San Jose State University. Ms. Bazavan received her CISSP in 2003.

Ian Lim, CISSP, is the director of Enterprise Information Security at New Century Financial Corporation. He is responsible for risk management and governance of all information security concerns in the company. He is the chair of the Information Security Steering Committee, which is composed of the company's C-level executives and directors from across major operating units such as information technology, legal, privacy, compliance, business continuity, and various lines of business. Mr. Lim directs the efforts of the Enterprise Information Security Department to develop and enforce corporatewide security policies; identify and remediate enterprise security risks; review and certify the security of architectural components; monitor and defend against threats and vulnerabilities; establish safeguards for technical, administrative, and organizational controls; and assure compliance with security-related state and federal regulations.

Previously, as a senior consultant in Accenture's global security practice, Mr. Lim worked in the healthcare, financial, government, telecommunications, and high tech industries to provide information security expertise in the areas of strategy development, architectural designs, process definitions, and organizational planning.

Mr. Lim is published, along with Ioana Bazavan, in the fifth edition of Auerbach's *Information Security Management Handbook*, edited by Tipton and Krause. He has also given security talks at the University of California, Irvine, in conjunction with the Association for Computing Machinery and participated in security roundtable discussions sponsored by Cisco. Mr. Lim received his CISSP in 2002.

Book Overview

Almost every book on information security will tell you how to handle security the "right way." What is lost between the lines is that the "right way" has unrealistic costs, assumes you have unlimited time, and takes for granted that you may not have the right staff for the job. In contrast, this book is about how to perform the best security for the best price in a real world with limited resources, pressing timelines, and real people. In this book, we will seek to demystify a range of common security practices or doctrines to highlight a "rubber-meets-the-road" perspective to the security problem. We will also give you frameworks, step-by-step processes, and benefits to justify a certain course of action, project management breakdowns, and other useful tools to help you in your implementation. It is our hope that this book will resonate with your experiences in trying to implement an information security program in a real-world setting fraught with limited budgets, understaffed teams, wavering executive support, end users who are difficult to please, snake-oil–selling vendors, and unrealistic auditors.

Our book is divided into five sections. Section 1, "Security Strategy—Thinking Practically," focuses on setting the right road map so that you can be most efficient in your information security implementations. In chapter 1, "Goals and Filters," we help you start thinking practically about security. This chapter outlines how to align your security objectives with the overall business need, how to filter myriad security opportunities into usable priorities that add value to the company, and why securing everything is not the answer. We then put these points together in chapter 2, "Building Your Strategy," by delineating the importance of developing a value-based and risk-centric approach to security strategy. Formulating a pragmatic security strategy is one of the best ways to reduce costs for your security organization. Developing a clear plan with appropriately prioritized projects, you can ensure that you are focusing on the right initiatives at the right times to support the business and minimize risk for your organization.

Section 2, "Security Organization Design—Cost-Effective Staffing," discusses the single biggest expense to the security organization: your head count. Once you have determined the right strategy, you will need someone to flesh it out and execute it. This section offers creative ways to staff cost effectively. In chapter 3, "The Right People for the Right Jobs," we discuss the security organization chart in general terms because each company has its own way of doing things and most already have an established department. We have created an ideal organization that is the basis for the remainder of the book. We draw parallels to a variety of real-world organization designs so that it is clear which of your people might fill the roles we describe. We then list a variety of roles found in the security organization and provide descriptions of their tasks and qualifications. We also provide suggestions on how to make the right staffing decisions if you cannot afford to hire as many people as you would like. Chapter 4, "Sourcing Solutions," takes the staffing model one step further and discusses the pros and cons of outsourcing to an onshore or offshore provider or establishing your facilities in alternate locations.

Once you have developed a strategy and hired the right people to execute it, it is time to get to work; as they say, "the devil is in the details." Section 3, "Security Management—Effectively Enforcing Your Strategy," puts theory into practice. Chapter 5, "Policies, Standards, and Procedures," discusses practical ways to build and manage the documentation that details your strategy. Chapter 6, "Training and Awareness," focuses on the importance of getting the security word out to the end-user community and describes ways to target audiences and time workshops to get the biggest bang for your training buck. Chapter 7, "Cost-Effective Audit Management," provides resources for operationalizing perhaps the biggest resource drain on your organization today: the annual audits. Finally, in chapter 8, "Reporting Your Value," we show you how to advertise your accomplishments effectively. After all, departments that can demonstrate how they add value get to keep and grow their funding.

Policies, processes, strategies, and training are crucial to the success of your program. However, in the final analysis, security is largely technology based, so you must address the technologies because that is where your least visible threats tend to lie. Section 4, "Security

Technologies—Establishing a Sound Foundation," focuses on this. In chapter 9, "Risk Assessment," we outline how to identify and prioritize high-risk areas to focus your limited resources on addressing the most imminent and severe threats to your enterprise. The risk assessment is conducted on an annual basis, preferably in the third quarter so that you can work remediation activities into the following year's planning and budget. Chapter 10, "Security Design Review," discusses the importance and process of reviewing projects and infrastructure components to assess their security integrity throughout the development life cycle. Chapter 11, "Exploit Protection," discusses how to mitigate efficiently the vulnerabilities that are common attack vectors in our highly connected world.

Section 5, "Security Operations—Maintaining Security Efficiently," is centered on the fact that security is not a one-time activity. Rather, it is an ongoing process. Once you have defined your strategy, made it practical through policies and other management documentation, and designed the technical components to support it, you need to bring the associated activities into operation. Making security tasks operational ensures that they are repeatable so that it is easy to maintain your more secure posture over time. Because repeatable tasks can be performed by a less skilled or otherwise less costly workforce, you can improve your security while saving money. Chapter 12, "Identity and Access Management," looks at the single largest and most complex operational component for most security organizations. It discusses how to manage the key controls provided by manual user management and how to automate user management tasks in a way that will make sense to your company and your budget. Chapter 13, "Cost-Effective Incident Response," reviews the other large and complex operational component in security: how to deal with security breaches when they occur.

By the end of this book, we hope that you will have gained a new mindset with respect to security—one that will enable you and your company to be successful in today's world of complex infrastructures, disappearing physical boundaries, and the onslaught of regulatory requirements.

Contents

SECTION 3: SECURITY MANAGEMENT—EFFECTIVELY ENFORCING YOUR STRATEGY

SECTION 4: SECURITY TECHNOLOGIES—ESTABLISHING A SOUND FOUNDATION

SECTION 5: SECURITY OPERATIONS—MAINTAINING SECURITY EFFICIENTLY

12 Identity and Access Management

Section 1

SECURITY STRATEGY — THINKING PRACTICALLY

One of the most common mistakes made by security organizations today is to be reactive and tactical in their work. This invariably leads to wasted effort, missed targets, and subsequent rework. In today's world of tight budgets and even tighter deadlines, it is critical that the information security program be carefully thought out and orchestrated to ensure that you are sequencing your projects in the most efficient way or, in some cases, the most necessary way. If you have a choice of being your most efficient or passing your next audit, you may opt to work on a few projects out of sequence rather than be hit with a significant deficiency or, worse, a material weakness.

Whether your priority is to pass the next audit, reduce costs, or improve your overall security posture, you probably have a lot of projects on your to-do list. By thinking strategically, you can ensure that:

- You have identified the synergies between disparate projects and can avoid rework or duplication of effort among them.
- You effectively prioritize the work to meet your security and audit needs as well as business objectives.

■ You have set yourself up financially. Many security projects have an up-front cost, but result in a net savings over time. If you are on a fixed budget and need to do more without additional funding, you may be able to divert the cost savings from one project to fund the next.

This section contains two chapters. In chapter 1, "Goals and Filters," we set the stage for using pragmatism to look at your information security program. We illustrate the importance of establishing a business-centric security charter supported by a set of security goals relevant to the business. We end the chapter with an emphasis on focusing on three pragmatic filters when you define your security strategy:

■ Filter one: focus on high-risk areas
■ Filter two: focus on creating and showing value
■ Filter three: focus on operational efficiency

In chapter 2, "Building Your Strategy," we show you how to put everything together and build a sound security strategy by selecting and prioritizing pragmatic security initiatives that are meaningful to the business, efficient in their use of resources, and that result in compliance.

Chapter 1

Goals and Filters

You Cannot Secure Everything

The first thing to realize in developing a pragmatic approach to information security is that you cannot secure everything. Many people are familiar with industry-recognized security control frameworks such as COBiT (control objectives for information and related technology) and ISO 17799, which stress a holistic approach to information security. Although these frameworks are theoretically sound, there is a gap between real-world implementations and the ideals set by these standards. The difference between a rookie and an expert information security practitioner is that the latter uses a pragmatic filter to extrapolate and focus on the applicable components of these comprehensive frameworks to align with the organization's business strategy, resource limitations, audit context, and corporate-political climate. We are basically attacking the mindset of building an information security program that tries to do a little of everything but misses the point of managing security risks in a real world. The following list describes the top five reasons why securing everything is *not* an option in the real world.

> Reason 1: Everything becomes a high priority. When everything is a high priority, nothing is a high priority. The inability to prioritize will lead to the mismanagement of resources as well

as curb progress on addressing high-risk areas. While you are trying to patch every hole in your environment, the next virus outbreak or information theft incident will strike at the heart of your operation because you were too busy to identify and dedicate resources to remediate the more critical vulnerabilities.

Reason 2: You will be spread too thin. To secure everything, you will need to start multiple streams of security initiatives. Each initiative draws from the same limited resources. Unless you have access to an unlimited talent pool that can complete initiatives in short order, you will find your information security program buried under a slew of unfinished projects that do very little to enhance your security posture or your image as an effective organization.

Reason 3: It will cost too much. You cannot secure everything because you cannot afford to spend irresponsibly in every security area. You would spend a fortune on tools and projects, and there would be the added, exceedingly large cost of hiring sufficient personnel to manage and monitor security tools deployed in the coverage areas. Also, you would struggle to find enough qualified people to hire. Security is a cost center in most organizations and must constantly prove value to justify its spending. You need to get the most for your money by focusing on high-risk areas as opposed to spreading your limited budget across the board.

Reason 4: It is a moving target. You cannot secure everything because everything changes all the time. Security risks change as the business takes different turns to accommodate a dynamic market economy. You will deploy solutions that become outdated when the environment that you are protecting is altered; in many companies, this seems to happen daily. The holistic mindset at the core of most information security texts today has a tendency to focus on coverage areas without a consistent methodology of reassessing new threats due to the changing environment.

Reason 5: It promotes mediocrity. Due to limited budget, skilled resources, and a time line, a decision must be made on whether to spend exceptionally in a few areas or spread the wealth across the entire operation. The latter will naturally result in lower quality implementations because of the resource constraints. The approach to cover every area leads to a culture of mediocrity in which security products are not fully "baked" and appropriate personnel are not sufficiently allocated to provide coverage for all the various products.

What Is Information Security?

Most security books will tell you that information security is about confidentiality, integrity, and availability. We will not argue with these tried-and-true doctrines, but our goal is to approach the security problem from a more pragmatic angle. Why is your company investing time and resources in the information security program? Essentially, management recognizes that this is the cost of doing business in a highly connected world. What, then, do they expect from you as an information security professional?

We would posit that they would like you to use as little money as possible to ensure that the proper controls are in place to prevent major security incidents and to comply with regulatory requirements. From that we draw out the following charter for a pragmatic information security program: "to enable the business to meet its goals in a secure manner in which regulatory and security requirements are met by incorporating appropriate controls, managing risks, and cultivating a security-conscious culture." To support this charter, your department should have the following goals:

- Help the business meet its objectives in a secure, cost-effective, and efficient way.
- Ensure minimal downtime to business critical functions due to security incidents.
- Ensure minimal compromise to confidential data due to security incidents.
- Ensure compliance to regulations and external audits in the various information security areas.
- Provide accurate, relevant, and consistent security reporting and awareness.
- Ensure effective management of departmental resources (including personnel and budget).

The challenge is to meet these goals in a business environment with limited time, budget, and resources. To be successful, we must be pragmatic.

The Three Pragmatic Filters

If you cannot secure everything, how do you decide on what and when to secure? The pragmatic approach to information security begins by applying three filters to the decisions that you make:

Filter one: Focus on risks that can have a significant impact on your company.

Filter two: Focus on creating and publicizing the value of information security.

Filter three: Focus on operational efficiency.

Filter One: Focus on High-Risk Areas

The goal here is to identify the threats in your environment that can cripple your company's core business functions and essentially discredit your information security program. This can take the form of a devastating virus outbreak, a significant compromise of nonpersonal information, or not passing the Sarbanes–Oxley (SOX) audit. This priority forces you to think about security in the business context instead of undertaking security for security's sake. Are you aware of the types of threats in your enterprise that can deal a critical blow to your company's business operations or reputation? Do you know the types of threats that could entangle your company in legal or regulatory penalties? Do you know the critical systems in your company?

Many companies have suffered significant blows to their operations because their information security professionals did not have clear assessments or remediation plans for critical threats. Choicepoint, for example, spent $6 million in addressing the information compromise of 145,000 consumers' data.[1] Cardsystems is another example. Its compromise of 40 million credit card numbers resulted in the company's acquisition by Pay-By-Touch.[2]

The point of focusing on high-priority risks is to steer you away from doing busywork while you have gaping security concerns to remediate. You need to effectively determine the types of threats that can deal a critical blow to your operations by developing a systematic risk assessment methodology. The risk assessment should assess the security of IT core architecture, business systems, end-user computing, data repositories, outsourcing solutions, and nonproduction environments (see chapter 2). The next phase of the assessment is to prioritize your risks based on the extent of damage, business impact, likelihood of exploit, and cost to fix. The prioritization process should include IT and business management. The socialization of risk priorities helps the organization understand that resources to remediate risk are limited. You have the onus to present the risk accurately, but ultimately the business stakeholders must weigh their risk appetite and decide which high-priority risks to address.

Filter Two: Focus on Creating and Showing Value

In the real world, some people shine and some people stay in the shadows. People who shine get what they need to do their jobs and are recognized for their achievements. People in the shadows do their jobs but get passed over or displaced because no one knows what they have done or how they have added value. The ability to demonstrate worth typically leads to increased budget, better executive support, and improved collaboration with other departments.

Through this filter, you look for the opportunity to implement high-profile projects that increase the value of your information security brand. For example, consolidate disparate security services, such as a single-repository user sign-on or digital rights management, into a common architecture that can be used across the enterprise. A project of this nature would speed the time to implementation and simplify management for future projects by providing reusable security components. It would also make system sign-on easier for users. In turn, this will diminish the likelihood that users will store passwords inappropriately. It will also win you big points with the user community because you will have made their lives easier.

Security is not simply about risk avoidance. Numerous security-driven projects (such as password self-service and automated user access provisioning) can result in significant cost savings to the entire business. Security projects can also enable business functionality that would not otherwise be possible. For example, if the business does not have good Web authentication and encryption, it cannot execute electronic purchase orders. In short, you need to look for projects that can be promoted and perceived as adding value to the company.

To show and create value, you need to develop an effective reporting strategy. Business executives have a difficult time understanding the value of security; they typically view it as a form of insurance or a cost of doing business. A successful reporting strategy helps them realize the criticality of information security in enabling the organization to meet its business objectives. The goal of executive-level security reporting is to provide accurate, consistent, and relevant metrics that help executives understand how security can help further their business agenda, thereby enabling them to make accurate and relevant business decisions.

Another key component of creating and showing value is to implement an effective security awareness program. Awareness extends the visibility of the information security value to the entire organization. Positive publicity increases the level of compliance and cooperation, which in turn increases the degree of security posture. The mantra of any security awareness campaign is that security (as well as privacy in many companies) is everyone's responsibility. However, most end users will not understand this without being told. Once end users understand why security is important and how their actions could have an impact on their computers and data as well as on those of others in the company, they will be much more likely to comply with security policies. If you have the buy-in and cooperation of your end users, you have taken an enormous step toward truly securing the company.

The point of this filter is that you cannot focus only on risk. You must focus on adding value to the enterprise and making that value known to executives, managers, and end users.

Filter Three: Focus on Operational Efficiency

In the real world of limited resources, you need to look constantly at what is consuming your time, money, and people. You need to ask the question of whether these operational or control functions are contributing to your goals of reducing risks and showing value. It is imperative that you develop an internal mechanism to increase your operational efficiency through elimination, consolidation, automation, and innovation.

Elimination is the process of determining and removing unnecessary procedures, technologies, or resources that do not add value to your security posture. You need to evaluate all your administrative and operational tasks periodically to see whether they actually reduce risks significantly. Conduct a cost–benefit analysis to see whether the effort outweighs the risk and systematically eliminate nonproductive tasks. This exercise typically weeds out a range of legacy processes that run on autopilot mode. "Because we have always done it that way" is not a good justification for why something is done today. An example of this would be to review and eliminate the need for a monthly war-dialing initiative of all phone numbers in your company when you have implemented network segmentation to protect your core business's critical systems.

Consolidation is the exercise of combining duplicative or similar functions to achieve economy of scale, increase efficiency, and promote consistency. Take a look at your operations to see whether you have functions that can be merged effectively. It is sometimes helpful to look outside your department to see whether you can absorb or forego duplicative functions across the enterprise. An example would be to leverage or combine efforts with the company's internal audit function to conduct security assessments.

Automation can be used to replace manual labor and create efficiencies in mundane and predictable tasks. By carefully selecting and developing repeatable tasks that can be automated, you have the option of reducing staffing costs or redeploying your resources to more critical tasks. An example would be to create an automated password reset and recovery feature as opposed to staffing up the help desk to address password-related calls.

Innovation is the idea of implementing well thought out solutions that cut costs while achieving the same, if not better, control of your security functions. An example of this would be outsourcing the intrusion detection monitoring function to achieve 24/7 monitoring, as well as to gain the advantage of interorganizational analysis and subject matter expertise on virus or hacking behavior. This may be a more cost-effective way of achieving a higher quality of monitoring than if you were to staff up internally for the same function, especially if your company is small and cannot afford to staff this function internally.

Eye on the Ball

Cost management is about achieving the right set of goals in the most practical and effective way. In this chapter, we have discussed the bane of trying to secure everything. We have instead proposed six security goals that will help you anchor your department to security objectives relevant to the business and three pragmatic filters that you should apply to making decisions. We will revisit these goals and filters in greater detail in the following chapters.

References

1. http://www.csoonline.com/read/040105/briefing_blotter.html
2. http://www.paybytouch.com/news/pr_10-15-05.html

Chapter 2

Building Your Strategy

Creating a Risk-Based Security Strategy

The goal of a security strategy is to identify the projects that need to be done within the next three to five years, determine their synergies and dependencies, align with overall business strategy and objectives, incorporate risk assessment findings, account for compliance requirements, and prioritize it all into an executable set of work plans.

It is important to spend an adequate amount of time gathering pertinent inputs and understanding their relative importance prior to formulating your strategy. Inputs for your strategy include business strategy, corporate climate, budget allocation, regulatory requirements, emerging threats, security pain points from previous years, and any other factors relevant to your specific industry and context. This allows you to prioritize your security projects more accurately. Be sure to document your prioritization accordingly. That way, if your decisions are questioned later, you will be able to justify your course of action. The weighting and prioritizing process that you develop as part of the risk assessment process (discussed in chapter 9) will go a long way toward helping you document your decisions in a standard fashion. However, the prioritizing process developed as part of the risk assessment activities may need to be extended to better meet the needs of a strategic prioritization because you will identify projects from other factors and not just from the risk assessment exercise.

It is also important to understand that a strategy is not written in stone at the time of creation. As you get to work on your projects, you will find that you constantly need to fine-tune the course because something does not work quite as expected, the business comes in with an urgent new requirement, or your company just made a significant move in the marketplace. The auditors may also dictate a sudden change or the initial direction of your security initiatives. For example, if the Sarbanes–Oxley (SOX) auditor finds material weakness in your file access permissions, you may need to formulate an immediate remediation strategy, followed by a full deployment of administrative and technical controls around file access.

Sometimes, you may need to change direction altogether; this could indicate that you did not do sufficient research and hopefully will serve as a lesson for the future. But even if this does happen, an efficient security organization will make the course corrections when they are needed to minimize the rework and added expense, rather than staying the wrong course and needing to dig out of a bigger hole later.

Providing the freedom to make course corrections will also help prevent "analysis paralysis." This is a situation that some companies encounter when trying to make big decisions: so many components need to be considered that the responsible team gets into a rut of analyzing them and cannot get to a decision. Clearly, the requirements will change over time, and the decision you make today is likely not the same one that you would have made a year ago or a year from now. But you must start somewhere—you cannot wait forever.

In the following sections, we illustrate the importance of creating a value-based strategy by helping you identify high-impact and relevant initiatives. We will discuss the importance of aligning with the business, keeping emerging threats in mind, and increasing operational effectiveness.

Creating and Showing Value

Filter two, as described in chapter 1, stresses the importance of developing an information security program that demonstrates value to the company. This is all the more important because security is typically a cost center for most organizations. Cost centers are there to support the main business at the minimal cost. If executive management and business units do not see the value that your information security program brings, you will eventually be looking at a shrinking budget and reduced support.

You need to promote the value of your information security program actively by implementing high-impact security initiatives, raising security awareness across the enterprise, and providing reporting that substantiates the value of your department's work. This chapter focuses on the high-impact initiatives. Awareness is discussed in chapter 6, and reporting is discussed in chapter 8.

High-Impact Initiatives

You have limited time, budget, and resources. Spending time on the wrong initiatives could have a severe impact on the success and perception of your information security program. A low-impact initiative is a project seen as insignificant to the company that has minimal effect on improving the company's business or operations.

In contrast, a high-impact initiative is about delivering security solutions that matter to the business. To qualify as high impact, the initiative must not only contribute to your company's success, but must also be perceived by the majority as a successful and worthwhile project. Pragmatically speaking, a good security initiative is relevant to the business, delivered successfully within budget, and well publicized to the executive team and management.

Understand Your Company's Goals

One of the cornerstones of a strong security strategy is business need. Every component of a company should be working to further the goals of the business, and security is no exception. You must be tuned into the direction in which your executives are taking the company. Prior to establishing your initiatives, make connections with key business players in your company to understand what drives the bottom line for your industry and how the company's leaders plan to make an impact in the near future.

If your company is focused on establishing its brand, the security tie-in would be in protecting the company's reputation from bad publicity. If the priority is the introduction of a marquee product, your security initiatives should be around protecting key processes that directly and indirectly support the viability of that product. If your company is planning to cut costs by jumping on the offshore outsourcing bandwagon, you should be focused on building a robust and secure remote access capability that facilitates the outsourcing initiative. Table 2.1 provides some common examples of how security initiatives can enable the strategic goals of various business units.

Table 2.1   Examples of Security Initiatives and How They Can Enable Various Business Units within the Company

Business Department	Security Enabler
Human Resources (HR)	Identity and access management initiative allows HR to provide targeted eLearning materials to users based on job function or seniority, providing more timely education to employees. Web security initiative allows HR to provide self-service facilities such as electronic pay stubs and online access to benefits, resulting in savings valued at hundreds of thousands or potentially millions of dollars annually (for large companies) because of not mailing pay and benefits information to each employee.
Finance	Public key infrastructure (PKI) initiative allows implementation of electronic purchase orders, enabling faster billing and receipt of funds.
Legal	Monitoring and event correlation initiative allows identification and prosecution of internal and external hacking attempts. Policy acknowledgment system allows enforcement of policy review and acceptance by employees; this can be used as evidence in sexual harassment cases.
Marketing	Implementation of a single sign-on solution reduces password violations significantly because marketing employees no longer need to remember numerous passwords to access the many systems they use.

By reaching out to the business units and learning about their business objectives, you can determine ways in which information security can help them better meet their goals. This will demonstrate to them the value that the information security department adds and may result in an additional source of funding; the business units may be amenable to providing funding to a desired security initiative to speed implementation.

It is beneficial to meet with the various business units to understand what they are trying to achieve for two reasons. First, it will give the information security department a preview of what is coming, allowing you to advise the business up front on security requirements to ensure that security is adequately built into their plans. Second, it will give you the opportunity to demonstrate to them how security can help them achieve their goals faster or better. Aligning your security programs to the strategic and tactical direction of your company facilitates better promotion of your initiatives because you can speak to the business in terms that it understands and cares about, leading to the aforementioned sources of funding.

Incorporate the Results of Your Risk Assessment

The second cornerstone of a good strategy is the risk assessment. During the course of a risk assessment, a number of projects will be identified. A lot of them will be technical in nature, such as the need for a platform-hardening initiative. Others will be procedural in nature, such as the need to better train system administrators in security practices related to the systems they administer. Still others will point to the need for an enterprise solution, involving new technologies and new processes, such as an enterprise identity and access management initiative.

Before formulating your new security initiatives, you need to incorporate input from your internal security assessment. The assessment should be done through the third quarter of each year so that prioritization of risk can be done in the fourth quarter. Tying your security initiatives to your assessment's findings brings relevance and significance to the assessment and your future initiatives. Additionally, the assessment's final report provides a communication tool for you to convey your proposed remediation solutions. Chapter 9 provides details on how to cost effectively execute a risk assessment that will provide meaningful results to fuel your strategy.

Forecast the Regulatory Climate

Almost every publicly held company in the United States has now experienced the impact of SOX. Regulations provide impetus for change and can typically fuel the importance and relevance of your security initiatives. Executive management is responsive toward regulations due to the potential for bad publicity, increased scrutiny, and regulatory penalties, which with SOX include the possibility of jail time for key executives. Be cognizant of pending security- or privacy-related regulations so that you can increase the relevance and timeliness of your initiatives. For example, following the success of Senate bill 1386 (disclosure of data theft for California residents), several identity theft protection bills are pending at the national level:

- S. 751, the *Notification of Risk to Personal Data Act*, requires notification of data theft incidents to consumers nationwide.
- S. 768, the *Comprehensive Identity Theft Prevention Act*, creates an Office of Identity Theft within the Federal Trade Commission (FTC) and authorizes the office to take civil enforcement actions against those who participate in the unauthorized acquisition of, or the intention to share, an individual's sensitive personal information.
- S. 1332, the *Personal Data Privacy and Security Act of 2005*, is a bill that addresses identity theft, data broker security standards, customer notification, and appropriate use of social security numbers.
- S. 1326, also the *Notification of Risk to Personal Data Act*, applies only to electronic data and requires companies to notify affected individuals when their personal data is compromised.

The final cornerstone of a solid strategy is compliance. But just as it is not beneficial to undertake security for security's sake, it is not beneficial to undertake it with the intent of being compliant. Being compliant is not synonymous with being secure, and if you are focused only on passing the next audit, you are missing the mark because you are likely focused too narrowly. Thus, you achieve compliance with today's regulations, and maybe you have even done some forecasting and have taken into consideration legislation on the near horizon. But what happens in a couple of years when still more laws get passed, or when current laws are amended? Do you start all over again and implement yet another set of processes and technologies to become point compliant with those, also? This approach is too tactical and will end up costing you too much time and money.

If you have a solid security strategy based on risk and business need, you can become secure, and compliance with current and future regulations almost will be a side effect. If you are secure, the only additional work you need to do to be compliant is perhaps to create some documentation or some additional reports to prove that you are doing the right things. If you are already doing the right things, documenting and reporting are simple. If you are not doing the right things, then all the documentation and reporting in the world will not save you.

Therefore, theoretically, the need for compliance should not result in the creation of new projects. Compliance should already be addressed in projects that were identified through the risk assessment and a review of business need. Compliance may, however, contribute additional documentation or reporting requirements to some of those projects.

You still do need to consider security initiatives that preempt regulatory requirements when you design your strategy, and your projects should clearly highlight how they will address certain legislative needs. You can even promote your initiatives as a competitive edge over other companies who are ill prepared to deal with these new regulations. Think of the difference between companies that started preparing for SOX in 2001 versus those that scrambled for compliance in 2004. With the advent of privacy laws, security initiatives that promote a sound data protection strategy that incorporates encryption, database security, and notification will have a clear ring of credibility with executive management.

Consider Your Pain Points

Take stock of problematic areas that have revealed the weaknesses of your security program. Did you have a security breach? Did virus outbreak incidents occur? Were there noncompliance issues? There are definitely areas of improvements in every security organization. The key focus here is to distinguish between what is mandatory to fix and what would be nice to fix. To do this, you need to examine your pain points from the following angles:

- What was the business impact?
- What was the security impact?
- What was the root cause?
- What is the likelihood of this incident recurring?
- What is the cost to fix versus the risk exposure?

After careful evaluation of your pain points, formulate security initiatives that will minimize the resurgence of your high-priority problem areas.

Keep a Pulse on Emerging Threats

Keep up to date with information security trends by harvesting data from information security Websites, attending cross-industry security conferences, subscribing to security publications, or employing a security intelligence service. For example, at the writing of this book, identity theft, the surfacing of sophisticated malware (malicious software), and the rise of botnets (collections of compromised machines remotely controlled by a hacker or hacker community) have increased markedly. Evaluate the relevance of these threats as they pertain to your company. Incorporate the potential impact of these emerging threats into your security initiative planning.

It is also important to note what the media are reporting in the areas of information security. The results of an RSA study on what the media covered during 2005 in the area of information security showed[1]:

- Data security/security breaches (24 percent)
- Malware (19 percent)
- Identity theft/privacy (13 percent)
- Legislation/regulatory compliance (11 percent)
- Vulnerabilities (11 percent)
- Network access control/ID management (10 percent)
- Best practices (6 percent)
- Wireless security (4 percent)
- Hacking (2 percent)

By considering what interests the media, you can ensure alignment with the most prevalent or high-visibility threats in the "wild."

Focus on Delivery

Consider the time and resources needed to carry out your other security activities, such as policy governance, risk management, and day-to-day operations, before pushing myriad security initiatives. It is better to be successful in three major initiatives than to launch ten that are mediocre. Use the following principles when delivering solutions:

- Set the right expectations. Avoid over- or underselling your initiatives. Speak in pragmatic and relevant terms to key stakeholders and set expectations that you can meet.
- Establish a realistic project plan. Carefully gauge the work hours and resources needed to complete the job and set expectations accordingly.
- Consider the people factor. Security initiatives typically have significant impact on the end-user population. Be cognizant of how people might react to a new security mechanism and build an awareness campaign that goes hand in hand with initiatives that have an impact on the pre-existing work culture.

- Be cognizant of dependencies. Make sure to consider areas of your project that rely on other departments' or organizations' participation to complete. Address potential bottlenecks early or develop contingency plans that reduce the importance of unreliable resources.
- Promote, promote, promote! A project is only successful if it is perceived as a success. Market the benefits and relevance of your project incessantly to your executive team and management. Build a positive aura around the project and provide meaningful status updates to key stakeholders on a regular basis.

Being able to deliver and promote your security initiatives aligns you to the priority of creating and showing value.

Taking the Next Steps

In summary, a well-designed strategy is the road map that will guide you to where you need to go. The more time and effort you put into gathering and prioritizing your requirements, the less rework you will encounter down the road. You will also realize cost savings by prioritizing projects that build on each other, rather than spending extra time and money "putting the cart before the horse." However, you should not spend so much time and effort on the requirements that you are incapable of making progress. It is a delicate balancing act that is a little bit different for each company. But once you achieve it, you will be on the path to success.

By creating a well-thought-out strategy, you ensure alignment with the business, enable the demonstration of added value, minimize effort wasted on rework or duplicative tasks, and better ensure compliance. But a strategy is just a high-level vision. You cannot expect others to read and understand your strategy outright. The rest of this book shows you how to staff and organize your department appropriately to best execute your strategy, as well as how to detail your strategy in meaningful ways so that it becomes understandable and executable by your department and others.

Reference

1. http://www.rsasecurity.com/press_release.asp?doc_id=6305&id=1034

Section 2

SECURITY ORGANIZATION DESIGN—COST-EFFECTIVE STAFFING

Section 2 consists primarily of chapter 3, "The Right People for the Right Jobs." Although large security projects can cost millions of dollars up front, head count is typically the single largest ongoing expense that the security organization has. Project expenses tend to be a one-time cost, with some residual annual expense for things like product licensing and maintenance. But after everything is installed and running, you still need and will have a staff. Section 2 also contains chapter 4, "Sourcing Solutions," which focuses on how you can stretch your staffing dollars even further by partially outsourcing certain operational functions.

How you build your security organization will have an impact on what happens over time. If you lack adequate strategic expertise, you will continue to embark on projects that may not have the right timing or a broad-enough vision to meet business needs effectively. However, the organization will not survive if you have all thinkers and no doers. Chapter 3 takes a top-down approach, with the idea that if you hire the right person in the chief position, he or she will do the right thing for the rest of the organization. Each key security role is described in detail, with characteristics that are desirable for each function, as well as an indication of how those characteristics come into play. Chapter 3 also provides suggestions on how to make the most of your staffing dollars in situations where you may need two people, but only have enough budget for one. This concept is taken one step further in chapter 4, where we explore the pros and cons of insourcing versus outsourcing, onshore or offshore.

This section will be especially useful reading for individuals seeking to build a new security organization or substantially growing for their existing security team.

Chapter 3

The Right People for the Right Jobs

Introduction

It is surprising how many companies still have small, tactical, and largely ineffective security organizations. However, with the advent of legislation such as Sarbanes–Oxley (SOX) and the resulting detailed security audits, that is rapidly changing.

As with anything in the information security arena, security personnel can be costly—in part because their skill set is in high demand right now, but also because information security is still a relatively new field, so skilled personnel are not always easy to find. It is crucial for any organization to hire the right numbers and types of security professionals to ensure adequate security is created and maintained for the company and that headcount dollars are wisely spent.

This chapter puts on the operational efficiency filter (discussed in chapter 1) and focuses on how to build a lean and effective information security organization without breaking the bank. It outlines the essential security functions in an organizational framework that meets the departmental goals mentioned in the beginning of the book. It then aligns the functions to roles, details the recommended skills for each position, and provides guidance on how to choose between two or more skill sets if you cannot afford to hire multiple people.

The Essentials of a Security Organization

Organizations are created to meet a set of objectives. Chapter 1 listed the information security departmental goals:

- Help the business meet their objectives in a secure, cost-effective, and efficient way.
- Ensure minimal downtime to business critical functions due to security incidents.
- Ensure minimal compromise to confidential data due to security incidents.
- Ensure compliance to regulations and external audits in the various information security areas.
- Provide accurate and relevant security reporting and awareness in a consistent manner.
- Ensure effective management of departmental resources (including personnel and budget).

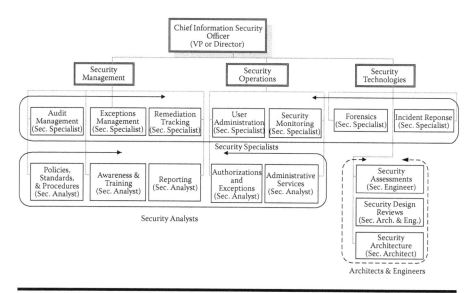

Figure 3.1 Organizational chart for a three-branch security department depicting how the positions of security analyst and security specialist span the branches. Only architects and engineers are focused in the security technologies area. This is a standard division of labor in a security department. Depending on the size of your organization, you may be able to consolidate further or may need to divide the areas more granularly, with additional management.

To meet these goals in a cost-conscious way, a security department must be organized effectively, and appropriate roles must be staffed accordingly. The organizational chart depicted in figure 3.1 provides a framework for organizing security functions and aligning security roles to meet the aforementioned departmental goals.

Security Functions

Table 3.1 outlines the three security functions, or branches, depicted in figure 3.1 and provides a high-level description of each functional silo. We will dedicate a chapter to each of the three branches of security, but for now let us focus on staffing strategies.

Security Roles

Six roles are outlined in our framework:

1. Chief information security officer
2. Security managers
3. Security architect
4. Security engineers
5. Security specialists
6. Security analysts

We will discuss each of these roles in detail and offer cost management tips along the way to help you make decisions as to how to staff your department with the right people for the right jobs at the right price. This chapter focuses on the individuals; chapter 4 also considers the possibility of outsourcing some functions to stretch your budget even further.

Start at the Top—CISO

The position of chief information security officer (CISO, or chief security officer, CSO) continues to be one of the most wrongly staffed in the entire security arena. Many companies have found that they had ineffective or even failed security organizations because they did not select an appropriate leader. The two most common mistakes that companies make when hiring a CISO are: (1) designing the senior security position to be at the manager or director level, when it should

Table 3.1 Summary of Objectives of the Three General Branches of an Information Security Department

Groups	Objectives
Security Management	Conduct periodic security audits to ensure compliance to regulatory and security requirements.
	Manage expectations and requests of internal and external auditors.
	Enforce security policies and follow up on outstanding security exceptions.
	Oversee remediation of risks identified by the security assessment initiative and/or security monitoring.
	Manage development, ratification, promotion, and maintenance of security policies, standards, and procedures.
	Provide relevant, accurate, and consistent security reporting to those who need to know.
	Develop and implement security awareness and training for the company to reduce the risk of security incidents caused by human factors.
	Build and maintain an easy-to-use knowledge repository to facilitate audits, knowledge transfer, and knowledge sharing.
Security Technologies	Conduct in-depth security assessments to identify and prioritize risks.
	Provide security reviews to projects throughout the project life cycle to embed security controls from requirements to deployment.
	Architect shared security components that are reusable, resulting in operational efficiency, cost savings, and architectural integrity.
	Design, build, and maintain security technologies across the enterprise to ensure that the security risks caused by human factors are sufficiently contained.
	Develop a computer security incident response team (CSIRT) to react quickly to security incidents.
	Conduct forensics investigations to retain evidence and/or identify root cause.

Table 3.1 (Continued) Summary of Objectives of the Three General Branches of an Information Security Department

Groups	Objectives
Security Operations	Monitor and control security threat levels to the enterprise at network, system, and application layers.
	Monitor administrative controls across the enterprise to ensure that security risks caused by human factors are sufficiently contained.
	Manage access and authorization controls for end users.
	Identify and elevate exception requests to management.
	Develop and update authorization lists on a regular basis.
	Provide miscellaneous security-related services to end users, such as answering questions, processing requests, and escalating issues as appropriate.

be at the senior director or vice president level; and (2) placing a very technical person in the role, instead of someone with strong management skills.

The CISO must be a senior-level person with strong management skills. At that level, no individual will ever be responsible for hands-on, deeply technical activities like architecting a metadirectory solution or conducting a forensics investigation. What he or she will be responsible for is making good management decisions between risk to the company and convenience to the business. CISOs will also be responsible for accurately portraying security initiatives and requirements to other senior executives, in an intelligible way. They will be required to fight for budget, educate the organization, ensure an appropriate strategy, and periodically assume risk on behalf of the company.

This position requires strong leadership skills first and foremost. Many companies have opted recently to put nonsecurity executives into the lead security position and have done so quite successfully. A good leader will easily learn security to the level appropriate for the CISO position. After all, the true security problems are not technical—they are procedural and organizational. Furthermore, a good leader will make the right personnel choices to ensure that other individuals in the group have the deep security expertise that he or she lacks, to provide guidance.

Bottom line: Having the right leader at the top will ensure the correct staffing all the way down the organizational chart. This will ensure that the company is getting the most out of its security head-count budget. If you are lucky enough to find someone with management and technical expertise, make that person an offer he or she cannot refuse. If you must pick between management and technical skills, go for the management skills.

The following characteristics are mandatory for a CISO:

- Proven management experience at the senior director (smaller companies) or vice president (larger companies) level is necessary.
- Strong written and oral communications: The individual should be able to negotiate with and educate other senior executives effectively.
- Demonstrated ability to maintain ethics and "do the right thing" in the face of negative company politics or pressure from other executives: Having audit, legal, regulatory, or law-enforcement expertise adds credibility to the role, but is not mandatory.
- Effective mentor and people developer: Implementing security initiatives can be rough on the morale of team members. It is important that the CISO be able to mentor individuals effectively through the rough spots in the interest of retention. The CISO's appeal as a "good boss" may also affect retention when other organizations in need of your team members' skills try to woo them away from your company.
- Confident decision maker: The CISO will be asked to decide the course of action on a number of risks and security initiatives. He or she must be able to research the available solutions successfully and make a clear and informed decision that will not be perpetually second-guessed.
- Fast learner: If your CISO does not have prior security experience, he or she must move up the learning curve very quickly. Even a CISO with long-time security experience will need to keep abreast of this ever-changing field.
- Experience in leading diverse, preferably multinational, teams: It is not unusual in today's business environment to deal with overseas locations, whether the company is multinational or has outsourced a portion of its operations. The CISO needs to understand how to manage members of a team that may not be physically located in the same place and may not have the

same cultural background. Diversity also comes to the security group in the form of skills and background. The CISO will need to be just as effective motivating a security engineer or administrator (someone with deep technical skills, who aspires to be a security architect) as motivating a security analyst (someone with strong process skills, who aspires to become a manager someday).

■ Ability to understand and defend the company's security posture and direction: Many CISOs today are faced with questions, demands, and criticism from a variety of audit groups internally and externally. The CISO is in many cases responsible for answering to audit findings and defending initiatives currently under way or potentially lacking. It is the job of the auditor to find something wrong. It is the job of the CISO to recognize when that something is legitimate and to push back when it is not.

Supporting the CISO—Security Management

The CISO will have one or more individuals reporting to him or her. How many depends on the size of the organization and, therefore, the need for security personnel. In a small company, one individual may wear several security "hats." A larger organization will obviously need a greater number of individuals that are more granularly focused.

At a minimum, the security organization will be split into roughly three areas: architecture and engineering (often referred to collectively as technology), risk management, and operations. These groups may be combined in a small company or further subdivided with additional management layers in a large company.

In general, individuals at the management level in the security organization should possess the following characteristics:

■ Some experience with security technologies: Security managers should have worked as developers, system administrators, or security process analysts (including doing product evaluations) at some points in their careers.

■ Strong management concept of all areas of security: Although he or she may not have deep technical expertise, a security manager should be familiar with security concepts such as identification, authentication, authorization, confidentiality, integrity, availability, accountability, and nonrepudiation, as well as understand how these concepts are implemented technically.

Security managers should also understand the concept of defense in depth and how that is achieved. Consideration should be given to individuals who possess and maintain a reputable certification, such as CISSP or the various certifications offered by the SANS Institute, although these accreditations alone are no guarantee of knowledge or ability.

■ Proven leadership skills: Security teams tend to have a greater variety of individuals than other IT teams, ranging from technical to nontechnical and from change motivated to stability motivated. As a result, it is especially important for security managers to have experience in managing and motivating different types of people. As will be discussed later in this section, it is not uncommon for companies to outsource a portion of their security operations. In that case, the security manager will need to have experience managing teams that include internal and external resources or multinational resources. Security managers also need to be strong motivators, to get their teams through the difficult projects, and to reduce the loss of valuable resources to other employment offers.

■ Ability to think strategically: The security manager will frequently be in the position to advise the CISO on what needs to be done. Although at any given time tactical work may be necessary and beneficial, over time running the group tactically will not be cost effective and the organization will not be able to make adequate progress on its objectives in a tactical way. Therefore, security managers need to be able to think from the perspective of how the business needs to be secured to meet its objectives (and be compliant).

■ Ability to design and implement policies: The information security organization will frequently be looked to in making policy decisions. Security managers should understand how to create and maintain appropriate policies for their companies, ensuring an appropriate balance between security need and business desire.

■ Excellent written and oral communications: Security managers will often be in the position to defend certain security needs and educate other departments—indeed, all end users—on the importance of security and the use of various security facilities within the company and its systems. Security managers will also need to interface regularly with most or all other IT departments, as well as with most or all business units to achieve their goals. Security managers with strong communication skills will benefit the company by educating those with whom they interact and obtaining their buy-in and cooperation. A security manager who lacks good communication skills could turn the individuals with whom he or she interacts against security and thus be a detriment to the organization.

For the remainder of this chapter, the focus will be on job descriptions in the three key areas (technology, risk management, operations), rather than on the exact management structure.

Technical Heavyweights—Security Architect and Security Engineers

The most technical people in the security organization will be your architect and engineers. A security engineer is someone who has deep expertise in the security workings of one or more ubiquitous technologies (such as firewalls, operating systems, etc.) and can make highly educated recommendations about the hardening and secure management of such devices. A security architect started out as an engineer (or possibly a developer), but over time and with exposure developed an understanding of how the various devices integrate into the whole of an infrastructure. Unlike an engineer, who is focused on a handful of devices and their secure operation, an architect focuses on the infrastructure as an entity and is able to synthesize the design of new enterprise solutions (such as identity management or public key infrastructure).

If your organization is small and cannot accommodate two new employees or you otherwise have budgetary constraints that limit you to hiring just one person, go for the architect. An architect has the background to do double duty as an engineer. An engineer may not have the broad thinking skills or be adequately strategy minded to cover your architecture needs. Granted, an architect's salary is higher than an engineer's, but your security organization's well-being hinges on having a solid architectural strategy firmly founded in the requirements of security, the realities of what is already in existence within the company, and the goals of the business going forward.

The following characteristics are desirable for a security architect:

■ Proven security engineering or development background is important.
■ The individual should have deep experience with key infrastructure components in your company, including platforms (UNIX/LINUX, Windows, mainframe, etc.), network (firewalls, routers, switches, etc.), directory services, and key applications (Human Resources [HR], finance, etc.).

■ Strong security background: Consideration should be given to individuals with reputable certifications such as CISSP or the various certifications offered by the SANS Institute, although such accreditations alone are no guarantee of knowledge or ability.

■ Demonstrated ability to conduct reviews and design security architectures for companies similar in size to yours is necessary.

■ Strong written and oral communication skills: The individual should be able to describe (verbally or in writing) architectural components and concepts clearly and accurately in a manner that would be understandable to nontechnical individuals. He or she must be able to describe the value of an architectural design to others.

■ Some management experience is preferred. The security architect may be an individual contributor, or he or she may be the lead of the security technology or engineering team. In the latter case, demonstrated ability to manage a highly technical group of people is a must.

■ Strong interpersonal skills: The security architect will be in the position to work frequently with other architecture and engineering groups in the company and will often need to impose certain changes to which other groups may not be immediately amenable. An individual who is overbearing or who does not have good negotiation skills may end up hurting rather than helping the security cause, despite being able to architect a solution correctly.

■ Proven problem-solving skills: The security architect is looked upon not only to resolve security issues, but also to provide innovative alternatives that protect the company and facilitate the business.

Desired characteristics for a security engineer include:

■ Deep technical expertise with the security administration of one or more infrastructure components that exist at your company (e.g., Windows/UNIX/Linux, network devices, directory products, etc.): Clearly, if you can only afford to have one engineer, he or she should have experience with as many components as possible, even though you may need to sacrifice some depth of knowledge. If you have the luxury of hiring multiple people, aim for individuals who have deeper and more focused skills.

■ Thorough research skills: One of the primary objectives of the security engineer is to conduct detailed technical research when new products are needed in the organization and when existing products need to be upgraded, hardened, or otherwise secured. The security engineer must thoroughly investigate the product in question and understand how it is used in the organization, what the product's business risks are, and how to mitigate those risks. The security engineer must not overlook anything that could later be exploited and devise ways in which to balance security with administrative overhead in a reasonable way.

■ Strong organizational skills: Another of the primary objectives of the security engineer may be to perform (or at least supervise the performance of) hardening activities. In a large company with many devices, hardening can be a project in itself, taking months to perform. The security engineer may require project management skills to ensure all devices are accounted for and adequately hardened.

■ Good written and oral communications: The security engineer will often interface with individuals from other departments, such as system administrators and operations personnel. At large companies, he or she may not actually perform any work on production devices, but rather will interface with other engineers or operations personnel to ensure the work is performed. At a minimum, the security engineer must be able to gain cooperation from the people with whom he or she interfaces. A security engineer who is a strong communicator can promote security by educating administrators and operations personnel on the security features of the systems in their care.

■ Forensics background is a bonus. The process of conducting a security investigation to determine how a breach occurred can be very involved and quite structured. The depth of an investigation and the rules of evidence handling depend largely on the decision of the company's executives and legal department as to whether to prosecute perpetrators or simply stop an invasion from continuing or recurring. In the latter case, security investigations may be relegated to well-trained security analysts who may not have such deep technical expertise, but who can get the job done and are less costly to staff than security engineers. If prosecution is the goal or if the investigation is particularly complex or sensitive, it will be desirable to staff an engineer. Also, if prosecution is the goal, whoever is hired to do the investigations will need to have specific training and accreditation in court-admissible forensics-gathering techniques and chain-of-custody procedures.

Process Excellence—Security Analysts and Security Specialists

The security analyst role is the most varied of any in the security organization. A security analyst can do anything from researching and testing a new product to writing policies or procedures, executing risk assessments, or creating and delivering awareness training—and anything in-between. The security analyst position is one in which you can have a significant impact on your staffing budget because this position is the least expensive of any in the security organization (unless you send work offshore or otherwise outsource something).

The primary reason why security analysts are less expensive is that they tend to be more junior, and the process and junior technology spaces are where you can hire entry-level people. This is how consulting companies generally work: hire straight out of college (or with minimal work experience) at an entry-level salary, invest a little extra in training, and voila!

Another cost-savings method is to hire interns to supplement the security analyst function. In any security department, mundane administrative tasks tie up valuable resources. The intern's role is to assist the higher paid analyst with menial tasks so that the latter can focus on activities that add more value to the company. Additionally, internship is an effective way of recruiting talent at a very low cost. This method of recruitment is superior to interviewing and hiring someone permanently in that it allows a full evaluation of a possible candidate's work ethics, interpersonal skills, ability to learn, and potential for growth.

Hiring "newbies" and training them has a number of advantages:

- People who are starting their careers tend to be highly motivated and interested in learning and making a good impression. You can count on eager employees willing to put in good effort.
- People who do not have a long work history do not have a lot of bad habits from other companies. By hiring someone who is just starting a career, you have the opportunity to ingrain the culture and work habits of your company in him or her. It is generally much easier to build habits into someone who does not have any than to try replacing old habits with new ones.
- Because you must train your young employees on their new tasks, you can train them the right way up front, to minimize mistakes they may make by trying to do something the way they learned from their last employers.

- At the end of the day, demand for security personnel exceeds supply. You may not be able to find anyone with experience, or you may not be satisfied with the few individuals who are available. You may get someone more quickly (and more cheaply) if you are willing to train.

The disadvantages of hiring inexperienced employees are:

- Eager, motivated people tend not to stay in one place for too long. You cannot count on these individuals staying with the company for years on end. This can be mitigated to a point by contractually requiring a certain period of service in exchange for the extra training provided.
- You need someone to train them. Ideally, you have one or two senior staff members who are good teachers. But if they are not terribly inclined toward teaching or are too busy to spend the time, you may end up with annoyed seniors and unlearned juniors.
- You cannot have full use of them from day one. Individuals who are fresh out of college or with relatively little work experience cannot be expected to hit the ground running. It will take time to train them to a level at which they can be effective.
- You substitute hiring dollars for training dollars. By hiring inexperienced employees, you need to invest heavily in training to get them primed for their roles. The disadvantage here is that they may spend your training dollars, get good experience, and move to another job.
- They require more hands-on management. Individuals starting their careers may need detailed supervision at first. Their manager will need to put more effort into establishing roles and responsibilities, coaching, indoctrinating the employee into the company's culture and expectations, instilling a good work ethic, and so on. If your managers tend to have a more hands-off style and expect their employees to "get it" with minimal supervision, you may have a problem.

The desirable characteristics of a security analyst will vary according to the role in which you wish to place him or her. Any security analyst should possess the following general characteristics:

- Some work experience is necessary, whether a college internship, part-time job, co-op position, or a more involved research project.
- Motivation, enthusiasm, and a willingness to learn should have been demonstrated.

■ Strong organizational skills: Most security analysts start by doing research or some sort of data collection or organization. They must be able to organize their findings or results effectively.

■ Good writing skills: For an analyst who will be placed in a process role, this is imperative. For an analyst who will be placed on a technical track, this is more of a bonus. But if you have the option to train someone "from scratch," encourage writing skills in your technical resources. As will be discussed in section 3, chapter 7, one of the key components to passing your audit is good documentation. But as most people know (or have learned the hard way), technical resources—those best positioned to do a lot of the documentation that is required—tend to be unwilling and in many cases unable to produce that documentation. If you have the opportunity to instill documentation skills in your technical security resources, do your company and the industry a favor and exploit it.

■ Self-starter: Above all else, your security analyst will need to "figure it out"—not only from a security perspective, but also possibly from a career perspective. Security is not rocket science; it is just common sense. Anyone can succeed in a security career if motivated to do so. An individual who is a self-starter will learn faster, be more thorough, and produce better results for your company.

■ Good communication skills: Like any security professional, your analysts will need to interact with other groups to provide and obtain information. For someone who is new to the workforce, the analyst will also need to be able to articulate training needs and progress effectively to his or her manager.

Some additional skills are desirable in job-specific circumstances:

■ If you are seeking a technical analyst who is interested in growing into an engineer and possibly an architect, look for a technical degree such as computer science or electrical engineering, or hands-on experience with one or more infrastructure technologies in your organization.

■ If your analyst will produce a lot of documentation (policies, procedures, standards, etc.), a technical or scientific writing background would be beneficial, as would someone with an English or other humanities degree that would have required a lot of writing.

■ An analyst who will be tasked with performing risk assessments or investigations or testing new products should have strong research and analytical skills and be able to synthesize usable results from large quantities of data.

The security specialist role can be seen as a maturation of the analyst role. Analysts who start out by filling a gap in a security organization gain specialized operational or technical skills over time. Analysts who excel in administrative and operational functions are good candidates for the security specialist role. Analysts who demonstrate strong aptitude for highly technical functions should be steered toward the security engineer role. You can also look for your security specialists outside the security analyst route. You can look inside or outside your company for IT-centric personnel who have a proven track record of running specialized operations and having a security focus.

The security specialist is an optional role depending on the size of your organization. You can achieve the same result by having different tiers of security analysts. In larger organizations, the specialist role identifies leadership in the operational silos, such as monitoring, user administration, compliance, and risk management. The following are some general characteristics that you should look for in a specialist:

■ The individual should have a specialized security skill and a minimum of two years of experience in that specific function.
■ He or she should possess leadership quality and the ability to manage entry-level personnel.
■ Desires stability and predictability over diversity in a career: The security specialist prefers to develop his or her expertise rather than to take a generic management route.
■ Pays strong attention to details and work in a consistent and dependable fashion: Operational excellence is gained through specific, reliable, and effective delivery of routine tasks. The specialist also must be responsive around the clock to issues that affect the business.
■ Big-picture oriented: The individual should have the ability to see his or her specialized function in the strategic and tactical direction of your department and company. You do not want to have a specialized staff member who is possessive of his or her silo to the disregard of your department's objectives.
■ Good interpersonal skills: The security specialist interacts heavily with end users and different departments within your company.

Operational Maturity—The Key to Successful Security

Security is a lot of work, in part because it is so broad reaching, but also because most security organizations are not operationally mature. A large company (or government entity) may have hundreds of thousands of employees, tens of thousands of computing devices (from desktop computers to border routers), hundreds of applications, and dozens of external interfaces, all of which need to be secured adequately. Then consider the maintenance aspect. Every day a new exploit comes out. What was secure yesterday may be insecure today. Thus, it is not adequate to secure something once. Security is an ongoing process, not a one-time event. Clearly, the operational arm of your security organization will be the largest.

The operations organization is typically led by technically oriented security specialists with analysts under them. Depending on the size of your operational function, you may need to borrow or permanently staff one or more process-oriented security analysts to help with process improvements and documentation. The job categories that need to be covered in your operations organization are:

- Event monitoring and correlation
- User administration
- Risk assessment remediation
- Exceptions management
- Compliance management
- Security technology management

The common characteristic of operational personnel is that they are stability driven, rather than growth driven. Unlike other job functions discussed in this chapter, for which you will tend to hire individuals highly driven by promotions and "the next big thing," in the operations area you want to hire individuals driven by stability. Operations personnel are not necessarily interested in becoming managers or executives or in having their job description change dramatically over time. They are interested in being good at what they do, learning and growing with the technologies they support, and having a stable, reliable, predictable job. The very nature of operations requires tenure because, ultimately, effective operations are based not only on knowledge of the technologies in use, but also on the politics, history, and idiosyncrasies of those technologies as they have been applied to your company. In short, the longer your good operations people stick around, the better off you will be.

The remainder of this section discusses the unique aspects of each operational job category in greater detail.

Event Monitoring and Correlation

With the advent of SOX auditing, the area of security monitoring has suddenly become much more important. Historically, many companies have opted to keep monitoring and event correlation to a minimum because collecting and analyzing audit logs are resource intensive from processor speed, disk space, and personnel perspectives. Any company can easily produce gigabytes or even terabytes of log data in fairly short order. But then what? How do you sort through that mountain of data? What events are relevant? How do you handle correlation across systems to understand whether the event in question was a single-user mistake or a broader hacking attempt? Who in the world wants to sit in front of a computer screen (or worse yet, with a huge pile of reports on the desk) all day and try to identify potential security breaches visually?

Clearly, monitoring is an enormous undertaking, and it really is no wonder that most companies have generally avoided all but the most basic monitoring activities. Unfortunately, avoidance is not an acceptable practice in the eyes of auditors, so most companies now need to do more—much more in some cases. To keep monitoring costs from exploding and at the same time ensure adequate depth and breadth, the following need to be done:

- Design a holistic monitoring strategy. As described in chapter 2, take the time to assess your environment and consider your critical assets, your high-risk areas, the expectations of your auditors, and the needs of your business. Ensure that your strategy is clear on what will and will not be monitored, and why.
- Select an event correlation and analysis tool that will work in your organization (of course, gathering requirements, going through a vendor evaluation, and conducting testing prior to purchase). Realistically, even if you hire an army of people to monitor logs and investigate events that occur, they will never be as effective or as efficient as an automated tool, especially when it comes to correlating events across systems, or identifying trends in a series of events that may happen fairly infrequently but regularly over a period of weeks or months. A monitoring strategy that includes an appropriate toolset, despite having an up-front price tag associated with it (and a potentially

large one at that), over time will save the organization money on head count and also will provide more accurate results. This is further discussed in section 4, chapter 11.

- Develop clear processes on how monitoring will be conducted. Document the daily, weekly, monthly, quarterly, and yearly tasks that must be performed, how they will be performed, and by whom. Also document the records that need to be maintained to demonstrate that monitoring is being conducted, the formats those records will take, and where they will be stored. A number of companies with decent monitoring practices have received audit findings simply because they did not have their processes documented. Despite the perception of documentation mainte-nance as a painful and distasteful task, it is nevertheless easier and more palatable than managing an audit finding. This is further discussed in section 3, chapter 7.

- Automate notification of events and scheduled reports. Instead of expending resources to monitor events physically on a screen, invest in a monitoring technology to detect anomalies and send meaningful alerts. Most security monitoring tool vendors today have invested in enhancing their reporting capability. Take the time to evaluate the type of reporting you want to provide and automate these reports when possible.

- Create and publish a perpetual calendar of monitoring tasks. This type of calendar assists the monitoring team in tracking its work and helps it ensure that it does not miss anything. It also assists management in verifying that monitoring is being per-formed as required. By being able to provide evidence of execution readily, you minimize the amount of time the mon-itoring team needs to spend with the auditors, and you avoid the cost of a finding.

- Consider outsourcing monitoring activities. The area of moni-toring is one of the most conducive to outsourcing due to its highly repetitive nature, the need for coverage as near to 24/7 as possible, and the lack of sufficient resources with the nec-essary skills in the marketplace. Outsourcing is discussed in greater detail in chapter 4.

Skilled monitoring personnel possess the following attributes:

- Highly detail oriented and self-motivated: Face it, monitoring is a tedious job. It is not difficult to overlook an event in the multitude that will occur each day or to lose interest. But that is exactly what cannot happen.

- Ability to identify the root cause of an event by correlating data from different sources: Basically, the monitoring team must classify a real incident from a false one accurately by looking at other detective controls and making the appropriate determination. For example, to classify an active network scanning event positively on your intrusion detection system (IDS), your monitoring personnel should be able to look at the system processes from the source computer to determine whether a scanning software is running, The other aspect of identifying root cause is to tune out false positives in the monitoring engine consistently to produce accurate and relevant notification of anomalous behavior.

- Ability to decipher event log contents effectively: Most systems, especially older ones, produce fairly cryptic event logs. It takes some amount of training to learn to read some of them.

- Understanding the security implications of an event: This attribute has two components. First, the individual that encounters an event must understand what the event means on that particular system. Beyond that, he or she must also be able to determine the security impact on a larger scale, based on other events that may have occurred simultaneously or recently, as well as on the danger posed by the event in the context of the company's infrastructure. For example, assume that your company only runs a Microsoft Windows 2003 server, and an exploit is attempted that affects the Microsoft Windows NT server. The monitoring team must first understand that the exploit relates to Microsoft platforms, but only affects Windows NT, so the company will not be affected. The monitoring team must also understand that this is nevertheless an intrusion attempt, and the potential hacker must be blocked despite the ineffectiveness of the current attempt.

- Knowledge of incident handling: The monitoring team may or may not handle forensic investigations when an event has occurred, but even if they do not handle the ongoing investigation, it will be their responsibility to take the correct first steps. This may include preventing additional events from occurring or enabling additional monitoring and allowing continued events so that more information can be gathered. This is in part a training issue, based on the desires of the company and the legal department with respect to prosecuting an intruder. But it is also a question of skill; the monitoring team needs to know how to handle the situations that arise and whom to notify about them.

User Administration

User administration is the other security operations area that has come under heavy scrutiny by auditors. Relative to monitoring, user administration involves perhaps fewer permutations of data, but a much more involved and complex architecture. Fortunately, companies have generally done more with user management than with monitoring, so there tends to be less of a gap to fill. Nevertheless, problems persist, as evidenced by the continued growth and profitability within the identity and access management market space.

Similar to monitoring, a cohesive strategy must be developed around identity management, with the focus on standardizing user permissions based on roles and rules; having tighter control of user movement through the organization (transfers and terminations); better ensuring segregation of duties; eliminating the use of shared or generic accounts; validating the ownership, use, and privileges of system and service accounts; and providing faster provisioning to accommodate business need and reduce the advent of account sharing. Because identity management is so broad, touching potentially every aspect of a company's infrastructure as well as every employee and a number of nonemployees associated with the company, identity management is discussed in section 5, chapter 12. For the purposes of this chapter, the discussion will be limited to the skill sets needed on the operational team that deals with user administration on a daily basis.

At the highest level, two primary skill sets comprise the user administration team. One is the role of access analysis and definition, and the other is the role of access administration and implementation. Individuals in the role of access analysis and definition interface with the business to define access roles and rules for each department. For companies that manually manage user access, defining roles and rules makes it easier for nontechnical business users to request access (they can simply specify their title, rather than enumerating all of the systems that they need to use) and for access administrators to grant access quickly and accurately. It also makes it easier to audit user access to identify when someone may have exceeded authorization. For companies in the process of automating their user provisioning (or that have already automated), the maintenance of roles and rules is critical to the correct operation of their automated provisioning system. The beauty of automated provisioning is that the provisioning tool will quickly and accurately implement access to each user as it has been programmed to do. The danger is that if the tool is incorrectly programmed, all users will be provisioned in error.

Individuals in the role of access administration and implementation are responsible for physically granting and removing access to systems. These individuals must have a clear understanding of the systems that they administer and must manage their workload to ensure that access is granted (and removed) in a timely manner.

Regardless of which role an individual plays on the user administration team, he or she must possess the following characteristics:

- Detail oriented: At best, mistakes made in designing a set of access roles for a department or implementing access for a specific user will result in the user's having inadequate access. At worst, such mistakes will result in a user (or potentially department) exceeding the intended authorization, which could in turn result in damage to the company's business and an audit nightmare.

- Able to handle large volumes of data: Unless yours is a small company or you have managed to minimize the number of systems you utilize, the user administration team must manage innumerable permissions, across dozens or hundreds of applications, for countless users. If your company also experiences an average to high amount of employee turnover or you have a significant temporary workforce, it also means that the volume of requests coming to the user administration team is high.

- Excellent time management and prioritization skills: This goes hand in hand with the ability to handle large volumes of data. Most user management teams have more work to do than time in which to do it. As a result, work tends to get prioritized based on the squeaky wheel principle. Unfortunately, this is yet another concept that the auditors frown upon; by being more responsive to the pressure of users who are at the company and need new access, terminations and other cleanup activities tend to get overlooked because rarely will anyone complain that their access has *not* been removed. On the other hand, focusing too much on terminations and cleanups can cause users to get impatient and share IDs with their co-workers so that they are not idle while they wait for their access. This is also an audit no–no. Therefore, it is extremely important for the team to understand the need for balance and constantly adjust priorities to accommodate all needs.

- Strong understanding of the company's business and how internal applications are used: In most companies, the reality is that you cannot just hire someone off the street that has a user administration background and expect him or her to be fully functional. Each company is at least slightly different in the way in which it sets up and uses permissions on systems. Also, most companies have their fair share of home-grown or legacy applications that other companies (even in the same industry) do not have. Thus, a strong element of internal training will need to occur with any member of the team. However, each individual on the user administration team must have a fundamental background in user administration on at least some of the systems that he or she will manage, as well as a basic knowledge of the industry to which the company pertains. This is critical to ensure that your user administrators are able to provide regular sanity checks. Although the user administration team should never be in a position to approve access to systems, they should be able to identify key instances when approved access may be inappropriate and to push back on such requests.

▪ Experience with customer service: The user administration team is quite possibly the only group of people within the information security department who will interact with end users on a daily basis. As we all know, end users are typically not technically savvy. Their lack of understanding of how technology works often leads to frustration, which they readily take out on the nearest available support person. User administrators are particularly susceptible to abuse from their customers if an access was implemented incorrectly (or the user thinks it was implemented incorrectly), if the user is in a hurry and perceives that service was not provided fast enough, or simply if the user has not been given training by his or her department or manager and has nowhere else to turn for help. Therefore, it is imperative that individuals on the user administration team have a strong sense of customer service. They need to understand how to communicate clearly with the customer in an easy-to-understand, friendly way. They also need to know how to push back tactfully on the customer who oversteps the bounds, is too demanding, or becomes inappropriate.

▪ Strong problem solver: User administration personnel will frequently run into challenges. Sometimes, it is how to translate a user's description of what screens he or she can update into the underlying permissions that grant this ability; at other times, it is how to troubleshoot a user's access when he or she can no longer do something that could be previously done and nothing appears to have changed at the technical level. User administration personnel will need to be able to solve the problem—in some cases, quite quickly. They need to be able to identify a course of action accurately and know whom to engage for assistance.

Risk Assessment Remediation

We will discuss the mechanics of the assessment process in chapter 9. In this section, we focus on the skill set needed to staff the risk remediation effort. Many larger companies have a specialized risk assessment team—a small group of individuals responsible for conducting risk assessments on an ongoing basis, one application or system at a time. Depending on the size of the company and the risk assessment team, the results of the assessments may or may not be managed by the same team. Regardless, the management of risk assessment findings is an operational task. Over time, as assessments get routinely performed and findings get repaired, the management of findings should become fairly trivial. Initially, however, the risk assessment could produce quite a large number of findings that must be addressed.

As with any other operational task, the way to reduce the cost of managing risk assessment findings is to be organized about it. Design a standard template for documenting findings and use it consistently. Look for trends in the findings and address the trends at an enterprise level with the goal of being proactive, rather than being reactive at the individual system level. For all findings, be sure to do a cost–benefit and risk analysis for addressing the findings and prioritize the remediation actions based on the analysis. Where applicable, ensure that remediated items are incorporated into the appropriate build images or operational manuals to ensure that future systems of the same type added to the environment do not have the same flaws as those that you just remediated.

The skill set required by the individuals managing risk assessment findings is somewhat unique. Ideally, you can find (or train) one or several people who meet all the requirements. Alternatively, you compose a team of people who collectively have the necessary skills, and they work together to get the job done. The following skills are required for risk assessment remediation:

- Strong analytical skills: The individual must be able to organize and analyze large volumes of data.
- Thorough understanding of security risks and their implications: This is critical to the proper prioritization of tasks and the ability to execute a risk analysis of findings correctly.
- Strong organizational skills: Once the analysis is complete, a work plan will need to be generated to track the remediation

tasks that need to be completed. In the first iterations of any risk assessment, there can be an expectation that a significant number of findings will result in a large work plan. Task completion will entail not only execution of remediation actions on the target systems, but also any subsequent actions such as updating build images or documentation. The remediation actions must also be documented—who performed the remediation and when—so that adequate evidence is available for the auditors. Any individual involved in the management of risk assessment findings will need to keep track of this work plan and all resultant documentation.

■ Strong communication skills: Individuals tasked with managing remediation of risk assessment findings will likely need to interface with a large number of people to have the remediations completed. It will be necessary for these individuals to be able to communicate effectively with others, as well as negotiate things like due dates.

Exceptions Management

One of the fallouts of risk assessment findings and remediation is that some items may be too difficult, too expensive, or otherwise not worth remediating. However, these items cannot simply fall by the wayside. They need to be documented and tracked as exceptions. To maximize efficiency of tracking exceptions, a process should be created. Document how exceptions will be handled (how they are submitted, who must review and approve them, how frequently they will be reviewed, how long an exception can be valid, how and where exception petitions are stored, etc.) and create a form that others can use to submit a petition for an exception. Also create a log or repository in which to enter exceptions so that they can be centrally stored and tracked.

Once the process is in place, someone will need to be assigned to manage it. The key to making an exceptions process operational is to create a perpetual calendar. Similar to risk assessment remediation, exceptions will need to be tracked to resolution. Unlike risk assessment remediation, the resolution of an exception may take years to achieve. Exceptions take two forms:

1. Short-term exceptions are granted for a year or less. These are the more common type, and they are requested in situations in which it is not possible to remediate something easily (i.e., a

project is required) or when remediation depends on some other event, such as the sun setting or upgrade of a particular system.

2. Long-term exceptions are granted on a semipermanent basis longer than a year. These should be granted sparingly, and they are generally only appropriate in cases where remediation will be cost prohibitive for a fairly low-risk finding.

Irrespective of the duration of the exception, it will need to be monitored. For exceptions with a specific end date, the responsible party will be obligated to demonstrate closure of the exception within that time frame. Depending on the due date of the exception and the complexity of the remediation, it may be advisable to schedule some checkpoints along the way to verify that the remediation is on track. Even if the exception is granted on a semipermanent basis, an annual check still should be done to verify whether anything has changed that might reduce the expense of remediation or increase the risk of not remediating. If delays in closing out an exception occur, a review will need to be conducted and possibly an approval for the extension obtained.

The skill set required for the management of the exceptions process is similar to that for the risk assessment remediation process, although it is conceivably less involved. This is largely a project-management type of function that can be easily relegated to a security specialist who is well organized and has good communication skills.

Compliance Management

Similar to exceptions management, compliance management is largely a project management type of function; however, it is quite a bit more involved. In the brave new world of detailed security audits for SOX and other regulatory compliance and the scrutiny afforded to the information security organization around computing controls, it is advisable to have a central point of contact within the group who will manage the annual audit effort. This individual will be responsible for interfacing with the various information security groups to ensure that the appropriate reports and evidence are produced and then made available to the auditors on demand. This person will also interface with the auditors and possibly other internal groups (such as internal audit, or the compliance organization if that is separate) to understand any findings and ensure that these findings receive due attention and response.

The skills of this individual are not "special" per se. Like so many holders of the other information security roles, the person responsible for overseeing the compliance effort should be well organized and have good communication skills. However, due to the sensitive nature of an audit (in which a more severe finding can cause enormous headaches), it is advisable to staff a fairly senior person in this role. At a minimum, it should be a senior security specialist or perhaps a junior manager. He or she will need to have the confidence to stand up to the auditors when needed, as well as the background and knowledge of various compliance activities within information security to be able to validate whether the auditors have executed their testing properly.

This individual must be able to identify whether the manner in which the auditors are conducting the test could lead to incorrect or misleading results and ensure that the tests are revised accordingly. He or she must also be thorough and timely in submitting evidence and responses to the auditors and articulate in explaining information security's internal processes. In short, this person will be the "face" of information security to the auditors, and their impression of the entire organization will be heavily colored by their impression of the professionalism of this person.

Security Technology Management

Depending on how your company is organized, management of security technologies such as firewalls, IDSs and intrusion prevention systems (IPSs), and the log analysis tools may or may not be the responsibility of the security organization. Typically, these skills would be a part of the security organization in a smaller company, but in larger companies, even the security technologies tend to be managed by operations support personnel.

Regardless of which team owns the personnel in charge of security technologies, it is imperative that the individuals in charge of managing those devices know what they are doing. They need to be skilled in how to configure the devices correctly to ensure that they are performing optimally. Security technologies are also more frequent targets of attack; if an intruder can disable the IDS or IPS devices, then he or she has a better chance of getting deeper into the infrastructure before being detected or blocked. Therefore, the personnel managing these systems must also diligently and expertly harden these devices and take any necessary additional measures to protect them.

Looking at the Bigger Picture—Positioning Information Security

This chapter has discussed in detail how to staff the information security organization cost effectively, irrespective of the size of your company. You should now have a good idea of how to structure your security organization, based on the needs and size of your company. Just one question remains: Where should information security reside within the company?

The de facto answer to this is largely political. Some companies have information security as its own entity, and the CISO is a peer of the other CXOs. Some have the CISO reporting to the CIO. Some have information security as part of the larger operations support organization. Some have information security as part of the internal audit and compliance organization. Some companies even have the CISO reporting to the CFO or the legal department. If your information security organization is already established somewhere and everyone is comfortable with the placement, there is no hard and fast rule that you need to change it. However, some guidelines should be observed to ensure adequate segregation of duties and avoid the appearance of impropriety:

- Although there may be a matrixed structure between information security and operations support, these should be separate organizations if information security has responsibility for conducting risk assessments or monitoring security controls on systems supported by the operations group.
- Inasmuch as internal audit or the compliance organization may review the operations of information security, these should also be separate organizations.
- Wherever you may choose to place the security organization, ensure that it has enough visibility and leverage to do its job effectively.

What about Physical Security?

Most companies keep physical security and information security separate. Historically, this has made a lot of sense because there generally has not been any intersection between the two groups. However, as more companies integrate physical access and logical access into one device and physical security monitoring devices begin to be incorporated into the IT infrastructure, some companies are finding a benefit to combining the two security disciplines into one organization. This is something that should be considered and periodically re-evaluated.

Chapter 4

Sourcing Solutions

Reducing Costs for Routine Tasks

As previously discussed, a portion of your security organization needs to be devoted to strategy formulation, risk management, policy development, governance activities, delivery of security architectures, and so on. This is where you need to focus your staffing dollars. Security is a high-demand field, but still relatively new, so the number of true experts is small (but growing). The high-impact areas mentioned earlier require a broadly skilled, motivated, and driven group of people to navigate effectively through the ever-changing landscape of security.

The operational arm of security, as discussed in chapter 3, includes components such as user administration, log and event monitoring and correlation, maintenance of security devices such as firewalls and intrusion detection systems, and so on. These components require a stable employee base that is generally less driven to be promoted and less interested in change. Personnel in this area are looking for stable jobs that pay well and are predictable. Although it is imperative to get well-skilled people for your security operations functions, this is an area in which less conventional staffing models can save the organization a significant amount of money or allow it to hire more people for the same total cost.

Insourcing versus Outsourcing

You have two options for staffing: hire people as employees and keep your operations inside the organization or hire another company and use its employees. Which one costs less largely depends on your needs. For example, if your organization is fairly small, but is in need of 24/7/365 operations support, it may be more cost effective to engage a specialized provider. If you are a large organization that needs entirely dedicated resources only during business hours, it may be better to

Table 4.1 Pros and Cons of Insourcing and Outsourcing

Insourcing	Outsourcing
Pros	
Keeping your security posture and practices in house and not exposing them to any external parties	Can offer more services at a lower price, especially if organization needs 24/7/365 support
Dedicated team solely focused on the organization	No personnel-related overhead—someone else deals with performance issues, salaries, benefits, hiring and firing, training, etc.
Better control over the team—if you are not happy with someone on the team, you can put him or her on a development plan or fire him or her	Experienced team from day one
Better control over skills and training of the team	Benefit of up-front consulting, especially if you are outsourcing areas of security operations with which your organization is unfamiliar; the provider can assist in developing a strategy that makes sense
Cons	
Can be more expensive, especially if 24/7/365 support is needed	Exposing security to "outsiders" can be culturally unpopular, but is a risk that must be assumed; can be substantially mitigated by developing a detailed contract with provider, checking references, and ensuring it is qualified, certified (SAS-70 or ISO17799), and insured

Table 4.1 (Continued) Pros and Cons of Insourcing and Outsourcing

Insourcing	Outsourcing
Cons	
Significant personnel overhead, including hiring, firing, training, and career management	May be less continuity in service received. If providers dedicate personnel to certain clients, you interact with the same person or people. Other providers rotate their staffs on an availability basis. Some clients find it disconcerting and frustrating to work with a different person each time they call. However, if you have leverage or can afford the cost, some outsourcers are willing to provide dedicated resources.
If a new area for the organization, must build the team and learn together; this could take time that you may not have	Outsourcing of any kind can be culturally unpopular within the company, especially if it results in layoffs of personnel. This has to be very carefully managed. At a minimum, layoffs due to outsourcing can cause significant morale problems. In more serious situations, personnel may try to reverse the decision by placing excessive blame of problems on the outsourcing provider. In extreme situations, personnel may try to sabotage the operation to get the outsourcing reversed.

hire your own team. Table 4.1 provides some key pros and cons for insourcing and outsourcing.

Onshoring versus Offshoring

In considering alternative locations, you again have two basic options: stay in your primary country of operations or locate your new personnel in another country. The former is referred to as "onshoring" and the latter as "offshoring." Some organizations also use the term "nearshore" to refer to an interim state. Nearshore basically refers to a nearby country. For example, an American company that opens an office in Canada or Mexico could be said to have nearshore operations. Some American companies may also consider certain business-friendly European nations to be nearshore. For the purposes of this book, however, any country outside your own will be considered as offshore.

As with insourcing versus outsourcing, onshoring versus offshoring will be decided primarily on a cost–risk basis. Onshoring will produce a smaller return on investment (ROI), but is less risky. Offshoring can produce immense ROI, but carries more inherent risk. Table 4.2 summarizes some key pros and cons for onshoring and offshoring.

Table 4.2 Pros and Cons of Onshoring and Offshoring

Onshoring	Offshoring
Pros	
Lower risk. You are already familiar with the legal and tax environment in your home country, although these can vary by state or province in larger countries.	Higher ROI. In countries such as India, the Philippines, and China, the cost of labor can be as much as 80 to 90 percent lower than the cost of labor in the most expensive U.S. markets. In Eastern European countries it can be as much as 60 to 75 percent lower than the cost in the most expensive U.S. markets.
No initial cultural or language barriers and relative geographical proximity. These factors provide advantages when on-site management or technical troubleshooting is required.	Large pool of workers. Although this is changing, as of the writing of this book, the popular outsourcing countries still have many more workers than there are jobs available. You will likely get more than one applicant per position, and many will be highly skilled, experienced, well spoken, and dedicated.

Table 4.2 (Continued)   Pros and Cons of Onshoring and Offshoring

Onshoring	*Offshoring*
Pros (continued)	
Potentially fewer internal problems. A stigma is associated with offshoring because onshore workers feel threatened. Many have the perception that offshoring jobs are bad for the local economy. By keeping jobs onshore, this problem may be avoided, or at least lessened.	Potential tax or legal benefit. Certain other countries may be more business friendly than yours. You may be able to benefit from smaller taxes or fewer mandatory fees.
Cons	
Smaller ROI. In large countries with substantial regional cost-of-living diversity, there may be as much as a 40 to 45 percent wage discrepancy. In small countries with limited regional cost-of-living diversity, there may be as little as a 10 to 15 percent wage discrepancy.	Higher risk. Countries in which labor is inexpensive can have any or all of the following challenges: Less reliable infrastructure — countries may have more difficulty recovering from natural disasters Less stable governments — some countries may be more susceptible to political upheaval Less robust legal system — some countries may not have adequate laws to protect businesses
Similar legal and tax requirements. If you operate in a country that is less business friendly concerning taxes and regulatory hurdles, onshoring may not change this.	You may have some cultural and language barriers to overcome initially. The geographical distance may require extensive travel time for your senior staff. Initial review, training, and setup will require travel. On-site trouble-shooting during a management or technical crisis may also present unique challenges due to the time required to bridge continents.

Common Considerations

Whether you intend to insource onshore or outsource offshore, certain considerations will always apply. These are discussed in the following sections.

Get Appropriate Legal Counsel

Even if you are just opening another office in the next county over, there may be some legal considerations. Certainly if you are outsourcing or offshoring there will be contracts to review. You also want to ensure that you can continue to uphold your country's or industry's security and privacy regulations in the new location and will have legal recourse if those working with you cannot or do not uphold those regulations.

Design and Implement a Disaster Recovery and Business Continuity Plan

If your primary location is in San Francisco, you likely already have earthquakes covered in your disaster recovery plan. If you onshore to a small town in Illinois, the earthquake preparedness will be irrelevant, but you had better plan on the occasional tornado. In locations such as the Philippines and coastal India, heavy rains and flooding are a seasonal reality. It is possible that a significant portion of your team may not be able to reach the office for days at a time. These risks need to be mitigated to ensure that you are not jeopardizing your security operations.

Manage Internal Perception

Some organizations use alternate locations and staffing to expand into a new business area, with no impact on their existing workforce. Most companies replace a portion of their existing workforce with less expensive resources elsewhere. This can and does cause significant morale issues within the organization. Even personnel not affected directly by layoffs may feel that they could be next and may be resentful that their long-time co-workers and friends have been let go. This situation must be continuously and positively managed to avoid unnecessary attrition and stumbling blocks for the transition. It is not uncommon for personnel to blame the new workforce excessively for quality issues or project delays. In extreme cases, personnel may try to sabotage the transition to demonstrate to management that the new workforce cannot do the work, in the hopes that members of management will change their minds and bring the jobs back to their original location.

Train and Transition Carefully

In part to manage perceptions and in part to maintain the integrity of your security operations, it is imperative that the new workforce be adequately trained. Also, sufficient time must be allowed for a supervised transition before the new personnel take over.

Ensure That New Team Members Feel Engaged

If you hire an outsourcing provider that rotates personnel constantly, this will not be an issue. However, if you have dedicated personnel belonging to a third-party provider or ones that you have hired as employees that are in a different location, it is imperative to make them feel that they are part of the team. Invest in sending the CISO or the direct manager to get acquainted with the team, review the security strategy, and help its members get started. The investment of travel expenses will pay enormous dividends if the remote team builds a good bond with its manager and CISO—team members will be more productive and make fewer mistakes.

Understand Team Members' Culture and Ensure They Understand Yours

Each country has its unique culture affecting how it does business and interacts with co-workers and supervisors. You can group countries by region and expect rough similarities in their culture. For example, many European countries have similar practices, as do many Asian countries. But you should not expect that because you have done business in England, conducting business in Italy will be the same; nor is India like the Philippines.

If your company's or country's culture is significantly different from that of your outsourced employees, you will gain tremendous benefit from exploring those differences. Make an effort to understand their customs and behavior. For example, punctuality is highly regarded in some countries, but not in others. If you expect strict punctuality from a group of people whose culture does not value punctuality so highly, you may be highly disappointed or frustrated. Eye contact is another perplexing example for many. In some cultures, lowering the eyes is a sign of respect and submission, but in other cultures it is a sign of deviousness and inattention. To avoid problems, be sure you know which is which.

If you are working with individuals from a country whose primary language is different from yours, you are strongly recommended to learn a few words of their language. You will be surprised at how much of an impact you can have if you visit your team or send them an email using their language. This small demonstration of effort and good will is always greatly appreciated, and it is a good way to build a strong relationship with your team.

But, ultimately, your understanding, although it will help build a good relationship, is a nicety. The reality is that your offshore employees will be working for your company and your culture. Therefore, it is imperative for the success of your outsourcing operation to ensure that they understand your culture. Design a training class and have everyone attend it at least once. The class should include information about how to deal with individuals from your culture—the expectations in terms of salutation, punctuality, sense of urgency, use of slang, eye contact, and other important characteristics.

Look for Recognized Certification

Offshore outsourcers are beginning to certify their services using American or international standards. The most recognized security certification to inquire about when selecting an outsourcer is the SAS-70 Type II.

SAS-70, which stands for statement on auditing standards No. 70, is an American accounting certification that reviews internal corporate controls. There are two types of SAS-70: type I and type II. SAS-70 type I is a point-in-time certification that describes an organization's internal controls and recommendations on whether the controls are sufficient. Type I does not include the testing of controls. Type II includes everything in type I as well as testing over a period of six months. Requiring your outsourcers to have SAS-70 type II will not only give you a level of assurance that they are security minded, but it will also facilitate in providing documentation for your auditors.

A note of caution about this certification: Do not equate SAS-70 type II to sound security. The certification does not force compliance to a defined set of security standards. Instead, the company getting certified merely must state what it wants its control objectives to be and have the SAS-70 auditor (who must be a certified public accountant) verify against its stated control objectives. When you are considering an outsourcer who claims to have an SAS-70 type II certification, be sure to ask for a copy and review the control objectives, the comments of the auditor, and the results of the testing.

Get Expert Help

It is advisable to engage a reputable consulting firm that specializes in alternative sourcing to assist you. Consultants have the benefit of experience with sourcing for a wide variety of organizations of different sizes and from differing industries. They will be able to assist you in avoiding common pitfalls and will also be able to guide you through the transition. Consultants also bring to the table a variety of sample deliverables and templates, including contracts, implementation plans, procedural documentation, and disaster recovery plans; these can save you weeks of work trying to do it from scratch. The large consulting firms work with a variety of providers all over the world and can be instrumental in assisting you in developing requirements and interviewing potential providers to ensure that they can meet your needs. Remember, it is always more cost effective to spend a little more up front and get it right, than to try to fix a broken transition or implementation later.

Section 3

SECURITY MANAGE-MENT—EFFECTIVELY ENFORCING YOUR STRATEGY

In section 1 we discussed how to build a relevant security strategy with a strong impact that will guide your security projects for the coming years. However, a security strategy provides a framework that has to be built upon. Section 3 takes you through the steps necessary to flesh out the strategy to a meaningful and executable level by creating documentation and processes, building awareness, and learning how to show the value of your organization.

Your security strategy will be embodied in your corporate documentation. Chapter 5, "Policies, Standards, and Procedures," describes how to document your strategy effectively into a set of rules and requirements that can be used by everyone in the company in the execution of day-to-day tasks and projects. By clearly documenting the details of your strategy, you ensure that everyone in the company is working toward the same end goals.

Documenting alone is not adequate. To get everyone on the security bandwagon, you must increase awareness across the organization. Chapter 6, "Training and Awareness," describes techniques for creating a high-impact awareness campaign and aligning it with other corporate activities and occurrences to get your message across most effectively to the greatest number of people for the least cost.

Chapter 7, "Cost-Effective Audit Management," addresses one of the most significant resource drains affecting today's security organizations: preparing for annual audits. Most information security organizations are faced with multiple audits each year: the internal audit group, external auditors preparing you to pass the official external audit, and the official external audit. Each auditor will likely want information in some slightly different format, at different times. Auditors will also want to understand your control processes. You will need to explain your processes to different audit teams and, possibly, to different personnel on an audit team if there is turnover during the course of the audit. Chapter 7 explains how to make the audit process operational by documenting your controls and standardizing your reports—in effect, creating a self-service repository for auditors to access as needed, leaving you and your team to deal with everything else on your plates.

Finally, after you have successfully documented your policies, trained your user base, and operationalized your audit process, you need to be able to demonstrate to the company how you have added value and earned your budget. Chapter 8, "Reporting Your Value," describes how to create meaningful summaries and reports that will impress executive management and the business, and ensure that they understand that the budget provided to you was well allocated and stretched to the last dollar. By demonstrating your value to management, you help ensure that your next initiative will be well received and funded.

Chapter 5

Policies, Standards, and Procedures

Introduction

Once you have established your strategy, you need to codify it into your corporate security policies. As most good security texts will tell you, a security policy describes the "what." What does the organization need to do to maintain security? Policies are fairly high level, providing broad statements that indicate direction, without really providing usable detail. This is where standards come in. Standards are much more detailed and describe the "how." How will you harden your border routers and Windows servers? How will you name users? Standards can be technology specific (e.g., hardening or encryption standards), or they can be technology agnostic (e.g., authorization or password management).

Finally, you will need to produce procedures. Procedures are the most detailed and describe the "how to." They provide step-by-step instructions on how to implement your standards or policies. There will not necessarily be a one-to-one relationship between procedures and standards or procedures and policies. Some standards or policies will not have any associated procedures; others might have several.

The focus of this chapter is not to address the appropriate contents for any of your documentation. There are numerous security books that cover security documentation down to the level of statements you can use. The only guidance we will provide on content is from an organizational perspective, along with a few pointers on presentation. This chapter will focus mostly on how to manage your documentation efficiently because it will need to be reviewed and updated regularly. We will also discuss how to manage exceptions because it is expected that you will have exceptions to your policies and standards that will need to be addressed.

Terminology Primer

This section applies to policies and standards only because these are very specific in their intent and must be carefully worded. Procedures do not need to adhere to such strict rules.

Culturally, when we speak and write, we tend to "hedge" our language so as not to appear bossy or demanding. We say things like "you should" and "if you wouldn't mind." The natural tendency when writing a policy or a standard is to do the same thing. For example:

- Users should always lock their screens before leaving their desks.
- Where possible, all systems should be hardened.
- This policy contains guidelines on how to protect the company's systems.

Even some otherwise reputable security books have this suggested language, which is very problematic and could cause your auditor concern:

- "Should" implies a suggestion and therefore leaves room for interpretation: "It would be best if you could lock your screen, if you wouldn't mind, please."
- "Where possible" allows a lot of interpretation. Is "possible" based on someone's best effort or his or her desire to leave the office by 4 p.m.?
- A guideline is a suggested practice. Policies and standards contain requirements. It is not your choice to follow them or ignore them. You are obligated to comply, and failure to do so could result in disciplinary action, up to and including termination. Policies and standards never contain guidelines.

Policies and standards must contain very precise wording. The intention cannot be left up to the interpretation of the reader. These documents must contain very clear wording:

- Users *must always* lock their screens before leaving their desks.
- All systems *must* be hardened.
- This policy contains *requirements* that address how the company's systems will be protected.

In some more formal settings, such as military organizations, the words *shall* or *will* are used instead of *must*.

Some of you will find such a severe tone intimidating and will consider that this goes against your company culture. You can make the tone friendlier without diluting the key words by adding some explanation to help the reader understand the importance of the statements. For example:

- One common way that intruders can gain unauthorized access to the company's systems is by accessing a live system session on an unattended computer. To prevent this possibility, users must always lock their screens before leaving their desks.
- Hardening is the process of enhancing security configurations and removing unneeded facilities on a system, to reduce the risk of intrusion. To ensure the confidentiality and integrity of our company's data, all systems must be hardened. Please refer to the company's hardening standards located at <intranet link or directory path> for detailed requirements.
- Security measures protect our company and our employees from intruders that intend to do us harm by modifying or stealing our customer data or corrupting our systems to prevent us from doing business. This policy contains requirements that address how the company's systems will be protected to prevent a loss of reputation or business capability as a result of a security breach.

As you can see, the key messages are still very severe in tone, but providing some background information and setting the context help the tone still appear friendly and nonthreatening. The message becomes, "We're not mad at you, nor do we not trust you. We just want to do the right things to protect the company from the bad guys." If some of your employees happen to be the bad guys, then that is a different story. Your disclaimer about "failure to comply will result in disciplinary action, up to and including termination" comes in here.

Policy purists would argue that a policy should only contain the requirements and no extraneous "fluff" like descriptions and definitions. It is up to you to decide how much "fluff" you put into your policy; just be careful not to slip the word "should" into your fluff and also be cautious with examples if you choose to provide them. You do not want to give readers cause to think that your examples are the only situations in which the policy applies.

One common question that new policy writers, and indeed many management personnel, ask is, "How can we say that all systems must be hardened, when we don't harden all our systems?" This is why policy statements are general and refer to standards for details. The statement, "All systems must be hardened," does not in any way qualify what "hardened" means; it could be basic hardening or it could be extreme hardening. Indeed, you will not want to do the same level of hardening on all of your systems. That is why the policy makes the general statement, and the standard handles the specifics. In the standard, you can have different grades of hardening for each platform, based on its use, location in your infrastructure, means of connectivity, criticality to the business, and sensitivity of data stored. If the definition of "hardened" changes for each server, you may find that you do harden all of your servers or you are very close to doing it.

Regardless, there could still be something that just is not compliant with the standard and, maybe, cannot be. In this case, you still do not want to address it in the policy or the standard. The policy and standard need to reflect what you want most of the time. Rather than "hedging" your policy or standard with "where possible" to address noncompliant situations, you address them through an exceptions process. This is described later in the chapter.

Organizational Tips

One of the most challenging decisions for companies is how to organize their policies and how many there should be. There can be a lot to say, and there is always the fear that if a particular document becomes too long, the intended audience will not read it in its entirety. Of course, if you choose to go with short, readable documents, you may end up having many of them. At the end of the day, reading ten policies that are five pages long each is really no different from reading one policy that is fifty pages long. Part of this problem can be addressed through the creation of standards: relegate any detail to the standards and keep the policies to the broad requirement statements.

The following sections provide some suggestions on organizing your documents. Again, this section only applies to policies and standards. Procedures will be very task specific and are not mandatory reading for everyone. A procedure will teach you how to do a particular task. You will therefore only need to read it if or when you need to perform that task.

Policies

Policies are best organized by audience, then by purpose. At the most basic level, you will have a user policy and a systems policy. The user policy will be very basic, containing only statements that directly apply to a user, such as how to protect a password, how to prevent theft of hardware, locking the screen, using a token to read e-mail from home, etc. End users have no idea what hardening or Kerberos authentication is, nor do they want to know. Those requirements do not pertain to them, and having them in a policy that is addressed to them will be intimidating and confusing.

IT personnel, on the other hand, need to know the requirements for hardening and authentication. They will be responsible for reading the end-user policy because they, too, are end users. However, they will also read the systems policy, which will tell them what they need to know to manage their servers, databases, and network devices.

The information security department at most companies also owns the acceptable-use policy. This is another end-user–focused policy that addresses things like appropriate behavior, copyright, harassment, expectation of privacy, and so on. This policy could be combined with the end-user security policy, but is often kept separate because it really has nothing to do with security. The acceptable-use policy protects the company from lawsuits associated with copyright violations, harassment in the workplace, internal user monitoring practices, and so on.

It is recommended that you avoid splitting out your policies by the security principle or other similar methods. This results in the creation of an unnecessarily large number of documents. The fewer documents you have, the more efficient your review process will be. Most people will find it easy to locate and read one, two, or even three policies. If you have eight, ten, or more policies, you run the risk of people missing one (or several) as they go down the list.

Standards

Standards should also be kept to a minimum to facilitate the review and maintenance process. There will clearly be many more standards than policies, but consider that any given audience should be able to get the information it needs in the minimum number of documents possible. For example, consider access control as a subject for a standard. Access control has a number of topics, such as employee access, nonemployee access, role-based access, and privileged access. Some companies would tend to create a separate document for each topic, causing anyone needing to know about access control to have to sift through four documents, and burdening the standard owner with maintaining four separate documents. It is much more efficient to have a single access control standard, with sections that address each topic.

Life-Cycle Management

Unless you work for a start-up company that is building its security organization for the first time, chances are you already have a fair number of policies and standards in place. Hopefully, you have taken or will take the time to review them for appropriate tone and take the time to consolidate documents where appropriate to make it easier to manage them. This section covers just that—how to manage the life cycle of your security document. This section applies to policies, standards, and procedures on different scales.

For example, there will likely be many more reviewers and approvers of a policy than of a procedure. The life cycle presented in this section is intended to be flexible and scalable to accommodate the life cycle of any security document or set of security documents. For clarity, we have chosen to describe the life cycle in the context of updating your set of security policies. The same steps would apply if you were updating your set of standards or procedures or even individual policies, standards, or procedures.

The life-cycle management process is executed at least once annually, or any time a major change has occurred, such as the introduction of a new technology into your environment; the removal of a legacy technology; an upgrade to a platform or application; the discovery of a significant new risk; or a major business event, such as a merger, acquisition, or expansion into a new market space.

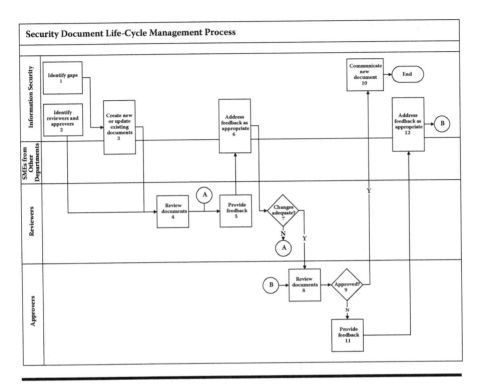

Figure 5.1 Security document life-cycle management process. Creating or updating a security document or set of security documents can be very time consuming due to the number of people that might be involved. One way to increase efficiency is to minimize the number of documents that you create to make the volume more manageable. The other way to increase efficiency is to follow an organized process, such as this one.

Life-cycle management is depicted in figure 5.1 and table 5.1 details the tasks depicted in this figure. The following sections provide context and background for the phases of the process that is illustrated.

Identify Gaps

In this phase, you assess your current policies and identify gaps. Gaps can take the form of missing statements, sections, or entire policies. Gaps can also be related to weak statements or findings made by your auditor. As part of this phase, you need to document and prioritize the gaps to determine which ones you will address and in what order.

Table 5.1 Process Flow Description Table for Figure 5.1

Step	Description	Responsibility	Deliverables
1.	Identify gaps Evaluate existing documents to identify whether statements, sections, or entire documents are missing. Create a list of enhancement needs and prioritize them.	Information security	Prioritized enhancement list
2.	Identify reviewers and approvers Determine who should be the reviewers and approvers for each update. Notify them that they will be asked to provide input. Provide an approximate schedule if possible.	Information security	List of reviewers List of approvers Standard contact memo sent
3.	Create new or update existing documents Make appropriate changes to existing documents, or create new documents, in accordance with the prioritized enhancement list. Distribute for review when complete.	Information security and subject matter experts (SMEs) from other teams (as needed)	Updated documents New documents
4.	Review documents Carefully review the materials that were sent and determine whether the content and wording are acceptable. Do not base an approval decision on whether or not the company is currently in compliance or currently performs what is documented. Approval should be based on appropriateness of the requirements.	Reviewers	Review completed
5.	Provide feedback Document all feedback and send to the authors or schedule a meeting to discuss.	Reviewers	Feedback documented and delivered

Table 5.1 (Continued)   Process Flow Description Table for Figure 5.1

Step	Description	Responsibility	Deliverables
6.	Address feedback as appropriate If feedback is legitimate, update the documentation. It may be more appropriate to make a change other than the one suggested that still meets the spirit of the comment. If the feedback demonstrates a misunderstanding on the part of the reviewer, consider updating the wording in the document to clarify because others may have the same confusion. Document a response to each feedback item—whether or not a change was made, and if not, why not.	Information security and subject matter experts (SMEs) from other teams (as needed)	Updated documents
7.	Changes adequate? Consider whether the changes made by the authors are adequate for approval. If they are, proceed to step 8. If they are not, return to step 5.	Reviewers	Decision on whether changes are adequate
8.	Review documents Carefully review the materials that were sent and determine whether the content and wording are acceptable. Do not base an approval decision on whether or not the company is currently in compliance or currently performs what is documented. Approval should be based on appropriateness of the requirements.	Approvers	Review completed
9.	Approved? Consider whether the documents are ready for approval. If they are, proceed to step 10. If they are not, proceed to step 11.	Approvers	Decision on approval

(*continued*)

Table 5.1 (Continued)   Process Flow Description Table for Figure 5.1

Step	Description	Responsibility	Deliverables
10.	Communicate new document Upon approval, post the final version of each document to a location easily accessible by all members of the target audience. Create and deliver communication messages to let everyone know that the new documents are available and that compliance with them is required. If needed, conduct training or track that the audience has read and acknowledged the new documents.	Information security	Documents posted Communication messages created and delivered Training and tracking activities executed
11.	Provide feedback Document all feedback and send to the authors or schedule a meeting to discuss.	Approvers	Feedback documented and delivered
12.	Address feedback as appropriate If feedback is legitimate, update the documentation. It may be more appropriate to make a change other than the one suggested that still meets the spirit of the comment. If the feedback demonstrates a misunderstanding on the part of the approver, consider updating the wording in the document to clarify because others may have the same confusion. Document a response to each feedback item—whether or not a change was made, and if not, then why not. Return to step 8.	Information security and SMEs from other teams (as needed)	Updated documents

Create New or Update Existing Documentation

In this phase, you task the right people with creating new policies or updating existing policies to fill the gaps. The right people will likely be information security personnel, but it may also be knowledgeable personnel from other IT teams or legal, or a combined effort.

Identify Reviewers and Approvers

Depending on the reach of each updated or created document, you may have a small or large review effort. For example, if you are updating the end-user policy to include requirements around using smartcards because you just rolled those out, the review process will likely only need to include someone from the smartcard team to validate the accuracy of your statements and, possibly, someone from Human Resources (HR) or your corporate communications group to ensure that the wording will be understood by the technically challenged masses. On the other hand, if you are creating an acceptable-use policy for the first time, you will likely need to review the entire document with legal, HR, corporate communications, and possibly certain IT groups as well. You may also need to identify levels of reviewers. For example, your vice president of HR may want to peruse a final version of the policy after it has been thoroughly reviewed by one of his or her managers.

Especially if the policy change will involve additional work for someone on their teams, more senior level people will want to have the opportunity to review your document after others on their team have had their chance. Similarly, you will need to identify approvers for each policy. Who the approvers should or will be depends on the magnitude of the change and the contents changed. All significant changes should be approved by the CISO, as well as other executive stakeholders. For example, a change to the systems policy may need to be approved by your vice president of engineering, also. The acceptable-use policy will need to be approved by HR and possibly your legal department. Depending on the stance of your legal department, *any* policy change might need to be approved by them, regardless of the content.

It is valuable to identify reviewers and approvers ahead of time and reach out to them to prepare them for the effort so that they do not be bottlenecks later.

Conduct Reviews

Once the documentation is updated or created, it will need to go through the review process. By the time you finish writing, you should have already identified your reviewers and the hierarchy that might pertain to them.

Start at the bottom. Work your way up the hierarchy, being sure to incorporate all changes from one level before engaging the next level. Document all suggestions in one centralized log (spreadsheet is the recommended format) and provide a written response to each suggestion: you incorporated it, you modified the text to meet the spirit of the suggestion but not the exact words, or you did not incorporate it for a specific reason. Be sure to specify the reason. This log should be accessible by all reviewers.

You will also want to keep a record of sign-off from reviewers to have evidence that they have indeed reviewed and accepted the final version of the document in question. Of course, you will want to post this evidence, as well as the revision log, to the audit repository described in chapter 7.

Interpreting "It Can't Be Done"

One of the common statements you will encounter during the review process is, "We can't do that." For the integrity of your document and the comfort of your auditors, always question that assertion. What does "can't" really mean? It could mean that a technical limitation of some sort genuinely prevents what you are trying to accomplish. If that is the case, explore alternatives. It could also mean any of the following: "We don't know how to do that," "That would be too much work so we don't want to do that," "We don't like change," or the reviewers may have misinterpreted your intention with a particular statement and they think you are asking for something other than what you are really asking. If it is a training or interpretation issue, this is a good time to get your security engineers or architect involved to provide clarity on the matter.

It is not uncommon for IT support personnel to be unfamiliar with security functions, and this could make them think that a task is much more complicated or time consuming than it really is. The "too much work" argument needs to be dealt with. It is true that security compliance adds to the workload of support personnel, and if they are already stretched to the limit, it is not fair to overload them. However, that is not a good reason to exclude a valid statement from your policy. Staffing is an issue that management must deal with to ensure adequate compliance. The lack of desire to change or do something new is also not a legitimate reason to omit a valid statement from your policy.

Obtain Approval

Once all of the applicable reviewers have signed off, you are ready to obtain approval from the designated executives. Here you must balance bombarding, overloading, and getting a timely response. Executives tend to be very busy, so you do not want to keep going back to the same individuals with one more, and one more, and—oh wait—one more. You may also not want to send your executives twenty documents at once. This is something to discuss with the executives once you have a good idea of how much documentation falls under their responsibility. Regardless, you will want to send the reviewed documentation to them as soon as possible and provide regular, gentle reminders to ensure that you get what you need from them in a timely manner.

Also, do not discount the need for iterations at the approval level. Most executives will not challenge a policy statement outright unless they do not understand the intent. You may therefore want to present the policy to the executive in person so that you have the opportunity to educate him or her and clarify the intent up front.

Communicate

Once your policies are approved, they are ready for posting to your centralized repository. After confirming that they are posted and accessible by everyone, create and deliver targeted communications to your audiences to let them know that one or more new policies are available and that they are required to read, understand, and comply. If compliance tracking is important, consider implementing a technology that can automatically contact the users, get them to read and acknowledge a policy, track that they have acknowledged, and even test the user on his or her understanding, if desired. Alternatively, you may choose to conduct mandatory training sessions and track attendance.

Managing Exceptions

In a perfect world, you would be able to come into full compliance with your policies and standards within one to two quarters. In reality, that may never be possible. A remediation may be postponed for any number of reasons, irrespective of how high the associated risk might be.

One common reason is that the risk is related to the use of a legacy system that may be on its way to being removed from the infrastructure.

For example, many companies still run one or more Windows NT servers with an older service pack because a legacy application will not function with the latest service pack or a newer version of Windows. Running NT with an old service pack may be a high risk, but due to the age of the application, the remediation to make it work with a newer service pack may be very time consuming and costly, or impossible. Executive management may, as a result, decide to accept this risk until the legacy application is decommissioned. However, once the legacy system is decommissioned, the remediation—in this case, upgrading the service pack or the operating system or even decommissioning that server—must be implemented as quickly as possible.

Another reason for a long-term remediation might be the need to implement an enterprise solution to address a risk. For example, one of your assessment findings may be that you do not do enough monitoring of events on critical systems to identify potential security incidents as they occur. You could, of course, turn on some logging functionality on various hosts and make a half-hearted attempt at periodically reviewing the logs, but this really would not address the risk properly. The most cost-effective and risk-effective solution would be to devise an enterprise-monitoring and event-correlation strategy and put together a program to implement it. But as we all know, this is not a one- or two-quarter endeavor unless you are at a fairly small company. Still, until you are able to implement your monitoring strategy, something must be done to address the "lack of monitoring" point findings, and the right answer might be to table them until the master solution is available.

In a large organization, you could end up with literally dozens or perhaps hundreds of point findings for which the right answer is to wait until later. The danger in this situation is that those findings are forgotten and never addressed, or they are not adequately documented, so the auditors get the impression that you have neglected them. The solution to avoiding these situations is to establish an exceptions process that will assist you in managing these long-term remediation actions to completion.

An exceptions process has four components:

1. The process describes how exceptions requests are submitted, what supporting documentation is needed for review, who reviews the exception and in what time frame, who approves the exception (this may vary depending on the risk associated with granting the exception), for what duration the exception

is valid, how an exception can be extended, how the exception and remediation are tracked, and what happens when the exception expires. The exceptions process should be documented using your company's official process template.

2. The request form is a standardized form that must be completed by anyone needing an exception. This ensures that all relevant information is provided up front so that time is not wasted in an ongoing dialogue with the requestor to obtain needed information. Figure 5.2 depicts a sample request form.

3. The response form is a standardized form that must be completed by the individual who reviews or approves the exception. This ensures that there is a formal communications mechanism between the information security team and the exception requestor. Figure 5.3 depicts a sample response form.

Sample Exception Request Form

(To be filled out by Requestor)

CONTACT INFORMATION		
Requestor Name:	Submission Date:	
Executive Sponsor Name:	Executive Sponsor Title:	
EXCEPTION DETAILS		
Please provide the name of the relevant policy or standard, and the applicable statement(s).		
To which device(s) or application(s) will the exception pertain?		
Please describe the exception you are requesting.		
What is the expected duration for this exception?		
What is the scope of the exception (e.g., number of servers impacted)?		
Please describe the business need for this exception.		
What would be the impact if the exception were denied?		
Please provide any additional comments you feel are relevant and list any attached documentation (e.g., technical diagrams).		

Figure 5.2 Sample exception request form. This figure depicts a suggested format for obtaining information from a requestor that is relevant in making a decision on whether or not to grant the exception. This form can be customized by exception type or left generic to apply to any exception. It is strongly recommended that this form be Web-enabled or added to an existing workflow tool so that the information can be stored electronically and metrics reports can be obtained as desired.

Sample Exception Decision Form

(To be filled out by Security Reviewer)

CONTACT INFORMATION			
Reviewer Name:		Decision Date:	
Approver Names:		Approver Titles:	

EXCEPTION DECISION	Approved	Approved with Modifications	Denied
Reason for denial (if applicable)			
Description of alternate solution/modifications (if applicable)			
Exception end date (if applicable)			
Security risks posed by exception approval			

Figure 5.3   Sample exception response form. This figure depicts a suggested format for formally communicating an exception decision back to the requestor. It is strongly recommended that this form be Web-enabled or added to an existing workflow tool so that the information can be stored electronically and metrics reports can be obtained as desired.

4. A tracking log contains entries for all exceptions. The log should include a numbering system for the exceptions and an indication of the content of each exception, who reviewed it, who approved it, when it was approved, when it expires, and remediation status. Figure 5.4 provides a sample exception tracking log.

Exception Number	Requested Date	Response Date	Requester Name	Executive Sponsor	Device/ Application	Approved (Y/N)	Expiration Date	Comments
Determine a numbering scheme to better track exceptions; include approved and rejected exceptions.	Enter date the request was submitted here.	Enter date a formal response was provided (approval or rejection) here.	Enter the name of the requestor as it appears on the request form.	Enter the name of the executive sponsor that is supporting this exception request as it appears on the request form.	List the device(s) or application(s) that are impacted by the exception as it (they) are listed on the request form.	Indicate whether the request was approved (Y) or denied (N).	Indicate the date on which the exception expires.	Provide any comments that are relevant to this exception.

Figure 5.4   Sample exception tracking log. This figure depicts a suggested format for formally tracking exceptions submitted for review. If the exceptions request form is automated, this log can likely be populated directly from the contents of the request form, with additional information manually input as needed. The first content row of this figure provides a brief explanation of the information that would be populated into each field.

A Question of Authority

At many companies, the information security department is in the position to authorize a wide number of requests, especially those pertaining to systems access. This puts information security personnel in an odd situation—in part because most information security organizations are not staffed to handle day-to-day approvals and in part because it is really not their right or their role. It is the function of information security to set overall direction: to write, implement, and enforce the corporate security policies. But on an individual basis, the approver must be the system owner. If the system in question happens to be the firewall, then information security is absolutely the right approver. If the system in question is the HR database or the accounts receivable application, then information security has no business approving. Approval for access to business applications belongs to the business owner of that application. Likewise, approval for IT applications or systems belongs with the respective IT owners of those applications or systems.

Therefore, it is in information security's best interest to set global policy and not get involved in individual situations and approvals. It should also be stipulated in the security policy who (in general terms) the appropriate approvers are for various types of systems and under what (if any) circumstances approval can be granted by someone other than the appropriate approver. It is imperative for any company to have a robust data classification and protection standard that focuses good attention on the details of the approval process and the responsibilities of those approvers. The data classification standard should also address how to identify approvers and business owners and the training they should receive. By removing information security from the daily approval loop, you not only free up some time for your resources, but also place the risk of approval where it belongs—with the business owner. The auditors will find substantial comfort in this approach.

Chapter 6

Training and Awareness

Introduction

The typical perspective of security awareness is that it is a tool to promote policy and compliance. We would like to propose that you look at security awareness as a key component of creating and showing value (refer to chapters 1 and 8). Value is a perception that must be honed by an effective security awareness program that accomplishes the following objectives:

- Promotes the message that security enables the business to function effectively
- Cultivates positive recognition for the information security program
- Perpetuates security principles across the enterprise, thereby increasing user acceptance and enhancing security posture
- Trains nonsecurity personnel to be ambassadors for security, thereby increasing security coverage without adding head count

Security is often viewed as a necessary annoyance due to its restrictive nature. An effective awareness program counters the negative perception and promotes the message that security facilitates instead of impedes business functions. Awareness brings to light the negative impact of security incidents, the high cost of reverse engineering security postproduction, and the long-term benefits of building resiliency and information protection in critical business systems.

Recognition is earned through publicity. When security initiatives are delivered successfully, it is important to publicize as appropriate to build credibility and garner increased support for the information security program. Favorable support paves the way for improved collaborations and higher rates of acceptance for future initiatives.

A significant number of security breaches or virus infections begin with exploiting human behavior, or social engineering: tricking users to click on malicious executables, charming a support representative to divulge useful information, or stealing a password off a Post-it® note in the victim's work area. Educating the user population in the importance of information security and increasing awareness of the social engineering tactics that others use to obtain information are crucial to battling the insecurities caused by human factors. Users who have an understanding of policy implications are also more likely to comply.

Launching an awareness program that incorporates internal security training also allows you to create ambassadors of security across the organization without adding personnel. An effective awareness program capitalizes on the fact that most critical business and IT functions have security components. By educating the business or IT end users to fulfill their security functions appropriately, you are leveraging nonsecurity resources to enhance your security posture.

Now that we know the reasons why security awareness is important, let us focus on identifying some guidelines to build a successful program.

Determine Your Key Messages and Target Audiences

In the planning stage, you want to solidify your key messages and identify your target audience for these messages. In line with your security awareness objectives, ask the following questions to root out your key messages:

- What value proposition do you want to make to different audiences?
- What security principles do you want to cultivate in your enterprise based on the input from your security assessment, knowledge of emerging threats, and pain points from the previous year?
- What initiatives do you want to push and how do you prepare your audience for them?
- What classes or workshops do you want to conduct to train nonsecurity personnel to fulfill their security functions?

Once you have established your key messages, build a table to map certain key messages to specific target audiences. Also consider what channels of communication you would like to use to reach your audience. From there, you can draw out potential events for each target audience. Table 6.1 provides an example of target audiences you might identify and messages you may deliver to them.

Table 6.1   Sample Listing of Target Audiences within a Company, Key Messages for Each Audience, and Delivery Mechanisms

Audience Group	Key Messages/Objectives	Communication Channels
Upper management	Report at a high level the major initiatives in information security Report on key security incidents Report on risk assessment and remediation activities	Executive reports Executive committee meetings Security memos Security assessment executive summary
Business/IT managers	Educate them on when to engage the information security department in their initiatives Educate them on the existence and implications of information security policies and standards on their initiatives	Webex training Security memos Workshops Handbooks and guides Presentations at departmental status meetings
IT personnel	Reinforce their roles and responsibilities pertaining to information security Establish their function in the event of a security incident	Webex training Security memos Workshops Handbooks and guides Presentations at departmental status meetings
Support personnel (helpdesk and PC techs)	Communicate how to protect against social engineering Educate them on how to report security or suspicious issues to the information security department immediately	Workshops Handbooks and online guides

(continued)

Table 6.1 (Continued)   Sample Listing of Target Audiences within a Company, Key Messages for Each Audience, and Delivery Mechanisms

Audience Group	Key Messages/Objectives	Communication Channels
All employees	Establish clarity on their responsibilities to protect systems and information assets. Communicate the company's acceptable-use policy. Convey where to find information security policies, standards, and procedures	Information security awareness week. Print and posters. Webex training. Newsletters. Intranet articles and sites
Nonemployees	Establish clarity on their responsibilities of complying with the company's security policies, especially as they pertain to customer confidential data	Nondisclosure agreements. Contracts. SLAs (service level agreements)

How you identify target audiences in your company will depend in part on the size of the company and in part on your available resources to conduct awareness sessions. Clearly, the more targeted and specific the training is, the more beneficial it is, but if you do not have the time or resources to do that, consider how to best target your messages at a higher level.

Create an Awareness Road Map

A road map captures, at a high level, major events throughout the year. It allows you to package your awareness program in one page. Using the target audience table you develop, plot each awareness or training event in a perpetual calendar format. Use figure 6.1 as an example.

Discuss your awareness plans with other departments in your company that do event planning. You may be able to time your events

Jan	Feb	Mar	Apr	May	June
▪ Publish Web content on Intranet site ▪ Security Awareness during the company's Annual Sales Event ▪ New Hire Orientation	▪ CSIRT Drill ▪ Update Intranet site	▪ Train PC technicians on supporting laptop security ▪ First Quarter Report ▪ New Hire Orientation	▪ Launch Awareness Week ▪ Helpdesk training ▪ Update Intranet site	▪ Identity Theft Awareness Initiative ▪ New Hire Orientation ▪ CSIRT Drill	▪ Server Hardening Workshop ▪ Second Quarter Report ▪ Update Intranet site

July	Aug	Sep	Oct	Nov	Dec
▪ Antivirus Awareness ▪ New Hire Orientation	▪ CSIRT Drill ▪ Update Intranet site	▪ New Hire Orientation ▪ Third Quarter Report	▪ Update Intranet site ▪ Data Classification Awareness	▪ New Hire Orientation ▪ CSIRT Drill	▪ Physical Security Awareness ▪ Fourth Quarter Report

Figure 6.1 Sample awareness calendar. This figure depicts an efficient way to organize your awareness program throughout the year.

to maximize impact and maybe share resources. Also be sure to set the expectation that your awareness calendar is a living document with flexibility and buffers built into the plan.

Keep It Creative, Simple, and Loud

Think of your security department as a new brand that requires considerable promotion. Model your awareness events after good advertising campaigns. Create a logo, a catchphrase, and a theme that can be instantly recognized as the information security brand. If you do not a have an internal resource for creating catchy artwork, go online. Various graphic design web sites charge a reasonable price to co-develop your logo.

Your catch phrase and key messages should be short, simple, and captivating. A good ideal to emulate is MasterCard's "priceless" campaign. The company used a punch-line slogan that follows interesting, humorous, and memorable scenes. Use attention grabbers and provide a link or a pointer for more details. One of the more effective tools to convey security messages in a condensed and effective fashion is the use of top-ten lists. The idea here is to abstract your important security policies into an easily digestible, short bulleted list with a reference to the corresponding policies. Figure 6.2 provides a sample top-ten list covering a variety of common do's and don'ts that should be communicated to end users.

Top Ten Dos and Don'ts

1. DO ... Safeguard your customers' confidential information.
- Compromise of customer confidential data has legal and regulatory consequences.
- Only use company information for its intended purposes.
- Never leave sensitive documents unprotected or in view when you are not around.

2. DO ... Protect your passwords as you would your ATM PIN number.
- Never give anyone your password, not even Help Desk representatives (they should never ask for it).
- If you suspect that your password may have been compromised, have the Help Desk reset your password (they will ask you certain questions to verify your identity prior to assisting you).
- Never use another employee's login or password, and make sure nobody uses yours.

3. DO ... Lock and password-protect mobile devices (e.g., cell phone, PDA, etc.).
- Activate the security features on these devices, such as password protection.
- Alert others in your department or office that this feature is available.

4. DO ... Use company resources appropriately – inappropriate use is monitored.
- There should be no expectations of personal privacy when using company resources.
- Unlicensed programs, pirated MP3s, games, or other software not specifically approved by the company must not be installed or used on company systems.

5. DO ... Ensure that vendors and contractors follow all information security rules.
- Regulations require the company to hold business partners responsible for the protection of customer confidential information, irrespective of who handles it.
- Don't allow vendors to plug their laptops into our network without prior approval from the information security department.

6. DON'T ... Open any attachments or e-mails that look suspicious.
- DO NOT launch e-mail attachments that are out of the ordinary, even if the e-mail came from someone you know.
- Report anything unusual to the Help Desk immediately.

7. DON'T ... Connect personal or non-business devices to the company network.
- Customer confidential data must only reside on systems or devices belonging to the company.
- Connecting personal computers or other devices to our network may result in virus infection.

8. DON'T ... Let strangers in with your key card access.
- Do not allow unknown individuals to "piggyback" entry into the company's facilities on your key card access.
- Visitors must get temporary badges from reception and/or a physical escort to enter our business suites.

9. DON'T ... Subscribe to non-business services with your business e-mail address.
- This causes unnecessary amounts of spam that slow down our e-mail system.

10. DON'T ... Think that the ability to do something makes it OK.
- Not everything has been disabled. There are some things that employees can do that are still a violation of our security policies.
- Accessing information on the network that is not needed for your job is a violation — even if access is not blocked.
- Your right to access the Internet can be removed if abused.

Figure 6.2 Sample "Top Ten Do's and Don'ts." This figure depicts a poster or print material that easily encapsulates security policies or principles into an easily remembered list.

You can also create targeted top-ten lists for new hires, new managers, programmers, executives, or any other audience that you want to address specifically.

Maximize Channels of Communication

A good awareness campaign gives the impression of ubiquity. To achieve this effect, use all methods of communication available to you. The following list outlines a number of communication channels that can be found in most organizations:

- E-mail can be used to mass distribute security alerts, tip of the day, promotional material with links to details, etc. Awareness is not just about publicity campaigns, but also includes sending appropriate memos to executives and management on security-related topics. You can also create a centralized mailbox for end users to e-mail questions, concerns, or even suspicious activity to your department.
- If your company has an Intranet, you should leverage this capability to build a central location for security resources. You should create an information security site that conveys relevant, interesting, and timely messages. Post headlines about latest security threats or security initiatives that will have an impact on the general populace. Dedicate a section to FAQs (frequently asked questions) where end users can get their common questions answered without tying up one of your resources. Create links to all your security authorization forms so that end users have easy access to them. Publish security policies, standards, guidelines, and checklists to encourage understanding and enhance compliance.
- The Internet could be used as an awareness tool as well. If you have public-facing customers, you can consider raising security awareness among them. Work with your marketing or corporate communications team to develop user-friendly security banners and warnings and guidelines for your customers.
- Use the print medium to publish posters, letters, memos, or reports to selected target audiences. Your awareness campaign could be greatly enhanced with a billboard or poster campaign that covers high-traffic locations within your company, such as near elevators, in the break rooms, and in the cafeteria. A caveat to using print is the price factor, so use it selectively. One good use of print dollars is to publish your top-ten list in poster size

and put a poster in every kitchen or pantry across the enterprise. You can also write selected memos or reports to appropriate executives to make them aware, get their support, or hold them accountable.

■ Training sessions and workshops can be used to educate some of your target audience to fulfill their security function appropriately. For example, social engineering is the act of manipulating human tendencies to gain valuable information or access to protected systems or areas. Conducting a social engineering awareness workshop will enable help-desk representatives and receptionists to be security conscious when answering phone calls.

■ Giving a short security presentation in other departments' status meetings is one channel of communication that is not often considered but can be highly effective. Most departments meet on a regular basis. Talk to the appropriate manager to invite you into a status meeting to discuss a security topic relevant to them. Expand this to committee meetings across the company or even sales meetings. Basically, capitalize on events where you have a captive audience and push your security agenda there as opposed to spending your budget dollars organizing security-specific events. Participating in departmental meetings has the added benefit of allowing those individuals to put a name and a face with information security. When they see a real person talking to them who is outgoing and concerned about their needs, they will be more likely to comply and participate. They are also more likely to think about security in the future and contact you with questions.

It is very important to use a variety of media in your awareness campaign. Communications personnel will often tell you that each communication will only be absorbed by about 20 percent of the target audience. Make sure to consider your audience. Sending e-mails to individuals who already get 200 e-mails per day will likely not be effective, but they may read a poster above the microwave while waiting for their lunches to heat up. Of course, if they see that same poster day after day, they will stop noticing it, so it is a good idea to change the microwave poster periodically or move it near the refrigerator. By having different mechanisms at different times to communicate consistent messages, you greatly increase your chances of reaching at least the majority of your audience.

Use Positive Reinforcement

Set aside some budget dollars for acquiring promotional giveaways such as pens, cups, shirts, or gift cards to encourage participation or generate interest at your awareness events. Be sure to incorporate your logo, slogan, and Intranet Web site in all your giveaways. Another effective way of reinforcing desired security behavior is to publicize and reward those who were exceptional in their efforts to secure the company. For example, take an IT manager and his group out to lunch upon a successful collaboration to deploy one of your security initiatives. Another example is to send movie tickets to help-desk personnel who detected and thwarted a social engineering attempt.

Be Opportunistic

Being opportunistic happens at two levels. First, be opportunistic in your planning. As mentioned earlier, make sure to talk to different departments in your company that have a public relations or event planning function. Try to collaborate with them so that you do not need to create your own security events. There are also departments, like Human Resources (HR), that have pre-established training programs such as business-related training, safety, sexual harassment, and so on. A cost-effective method to push security training is to embed a security component into an established training curriculum. For example, incorporate security guidelines into the existing new-hire orientation delivered by HR. Getting your message across to people as they walk in the door, when they are more likely to pay attention to make a good impression, is an opportunity that should be seized.

Second, capitalize on real-time or near–real-time opportunities to promote your security agenda. Security incidents that affect a majority of your target audience happen throughout the year. It could be an internal event such as a virus outbreak or a newsworthy incident that affects one of your competitors. It could be the publication of a new privacy law that changes how a company handles nonpublic information. Keep your awareness program flexible enough so that you can maximize the timeliness of your promotional events. For example, in your awareness calendar you had planned a virus awareness initiative in May, but a virus infected a number of employees in March. If you move the virus awareness initiative to late March or early April to coincide better with the recent virus outbreak, you will be able to take full advantage of your audience's frame of mind, and you will likely get much broader participation in the event. This is being flexible and opportunistic. Similarly, you could send out memos or e-mails following a huge news report on identity theft, reinforcing your security guidelines for protecting sensitive data.

Make Awareness Everyone's Responsibility

Security awareness should not be the sole responsibility of one person. You can have one coordinator, but every member of your department should participate to maximize the output of your awareness program. You and your coordinator should build initiatives and assign them to different members of your department for ownership and execution. You could also engage people outside your department to lead or participate in awareness initiatives. Last, you could push a "train the trainer" initiative where you require and equip nonsecurity managers to hold a security awareness session with their departments on a periodic basis. This allows for much more frequent delivery of awareness sessions than your department alone could handle, especially if you work for a large company that may have a number of locations nationally or globally. If you choose to go this route, however, be sure to audit these sessions every now and then to ensure that they are being delivered.

Chapter 7

Cost-Effective Audit Management

Introduction

The advent of auditing has been a mixed blessing for information security. On one hand, just about every security practitioner has been working many extra hours to implement a lot of new processes and technologies in time to pass the next audit; in some cases, auditors have been (or are becoming) unreasonable in their expectations. On the other hand, the processes and technologies being implemented are generally good for security, not just for passing audit, and the reality is that most companies would not be spending so much on security if it were not for the newer audit, security, and reporting requirements set forth by legislation such as Sarbanes–Oxley (SOX), the Health Insurance Portability and Accountability Act (HIPAA), the Gramm–Leach–Bliley Act (GLBA), and others.

Whether you like the new audits or not, the reality is that they are here to stay. As the auditors refine their methods and determine what they should look for, they will likely get tougher, and there will be an expectation of improvement over time. There will also be the comparison factor—the firm that audits your company likely audits your competitors, or at least some of them. There will be an expectation that similar companies have similar controls. If your company falls behind in a particular area relative to "industry average," you can expect the auditors to focus on that.

As most have already experienced, undergoing an audit is extremely painful. Most security organizations have multiple audits during the year: internal audit, external audit in preparation for the actual external audit, and the actual external audit. Information security may also have to assist the business in its financial audit by providing information or reports. This becomes an enormous resource drain. You practically must staff a small army of people just to deal with the audits and their findings.

Auditing for the newer legislation like SOX currently manifests itself in one broad fashion: the auditors are not yet sure of themselves. Because the legislation is so vague and Congress provided so little guidance on how the law should be implemented, the audit community has been forced to "figure it out." Thus, over the past two years, many companies have experienced possibly unexpected changes in the testing methodology. The auditors may have determined that the way a particular control was tested last year was inadequate, and as a result they will test differently this year. This in turn causes two additional problems:

1. A different or more thorough test may lead to findings that did not materialize last year. This raises a multitude of questions for everyone—executives, the board of directors, and possibly shareholders.
2. A different or more thorough test may lead to additional work for the information security or IT teams. There may be a need for additional evidence, or additional "massaging" of existing evidence for presentation to the auditors.

The good news is that, within a year or so, the refinement period should be over. The large audit firms, in particular, will have completed enough audits that they should have a pretty firm set of best practices. Now is a good time to begin implementing operations because you likely will not be faced with a lot of rework as the auditors continue to refine their processes. The bad news is that once the auditors finish refining their processes, the next step will be to go deeper. This will be the ongoing problem. Ultimately, the auditors will be looking for maturity. As their processes mature, they will expect yours to do the same. What may have earned you a passing grade last year may be marginal or failing this year. The auditors' drive will be idealistic: perfect control. We all know that is not possible in the real world; no company will ever come away with a perfect audit score, but companies will need to come fairly close.

This chapter outlines a three-step process describing how to bring the audit process into operation to minimize the impact to your resources when executing an audit, irrespective of who is conducting it. This chapter also focuses on how to ensure no misunderstandings on the part of the auditors that could lead them to an incorrect conclusion in their testing, so that the audit process is as efficient and cost effective as possible. As with most other things described in this book, there will be an initial effort required to get to an operational state, but the up-front cost will pay big dividends on an ongoing basis.

Step 1—Set Expectations

Most audits are a group effort. Information security will be solely responsible for producing certain evidence, but how that evidence is collected and delivered will often involve other IT or even business departments. It is advisable to meet with all auditors near the beginning of the year to get an understanding of their expectations. The attendees should include any involved executive stakeholders (such as the CISO, other IT department heads, the head of internal audit, the engagement lead for the external auditing firm, etc.) and the individuals who will be involved in the day-to-day execution of the audit—that is, the individuals from the audit firm (or internal audit) who be collecting and analyzing evidence, as well as individuals from information security and possibly other IT or business departments who can describe processes, produce evidence, or speak to deficiencies or weaknesses.

The auditors should be prepared to tell you what they will be testing and how they will be performing those tests. If they have previously audited your company, they should explain how this year's tests will differ from last year's tests, if at all. They should also provide a timeline of when they expect to arrive, when they will need certain pieces of evidence, and what expectations they have with respect to that evidence (format, etc.). Assuming that you conduct the meeting early in the year and most audits occur in the latter half of the year, the timelines will be highly approximate, but they will serve to give you at least an idea of what to expect.

By the end of this meeting (or meetings, if you have multiple auditors), you should have a clear understanding of what is expected of you by the auditors. They should also have a clear understanding of what you expect. The audit process is a two-way street, and the company should be driving the audit and the auditors—not the other way around. Contrary to popular belief, the auditors should not be telling you how to run your business. They may find weaknesses in certain processes that you will need to address, but it is not their place to dictate what you can and cannot do within the realm of reasonableness.

Likewise, their ability to dictate the content of evidence can be limited. Many companies spend enormous amounts of time creating ad hoc evidence reports for the auditors, at their whim. This meeting is a good time to iron out what reports will be created and when. You can set the expectation that, except under unusual circumstances, the auditors will not receive any special reports other than what you normally produce. This alone may save your resources a lot of time.

The expectations meeting should also address the communication paths between your company and the auditors. How will the auditors receive information they have requested? How and with whom will they validate and communicate their results? To whom do they turn if they have questions? How do they transition internally to others if there is turnover on their team? There will be recommendations on each of these items later in this chapter. For now, suffice it to say that these questions must be answered in this initial set of meetings in a manner agreeable to all parties.

During these "all-hands" meetings, or possibly separately, you will want to have some roles and responsibilities discussions internally. These discussions should delineate how the various IT and business teams will work together to make the audit run smoothly, to prevent miscommunications, and to ensure that different departments are not duplicating effort. The meeting with the auditors needs to occur first to understand their expectations. If you are unclear as to how you may work together internally to meet the auditors' expectations, you may wish to involve the external auditors in these internal discussions. Alternately, you may choose to leave them out of it and keep these conversations strictly inside the company.

The agreements made in all of these initial meetings must be very carefully documented. Get the best note taker in your organization to attend and take copious notes. Better yet, have a couple of people take notes to ensure that nothing is missed and everyone understood the same thing. Once the meeting minutes are documented and validated, they should be distributed to all attendees and also posted at some common location accessible by everyone (discussed in step 2).

For continuity, it is helpful to have one or more people who can attend all of the meetings assigned to the overall audit process. This person or team would then be in a good position to identify gaps or situations in which effort may be duplicated.

Step 2—Prepare Your Workspace

A common problem that companies face in communicating with the auditors is the use of e-mail. It is indeed quick and easy, but causes tracking problems. Did you send that report the auditors asked for? Did you copy Joe so that he knows not to send it? Oops—no, you did not, and Joe sent them a copy as well; the report dates are slightly different and now the auditors are confused. Did Jane forward you the audit responses that she received from the auditors because they forgot to copy you? No, Jane has already left for vacation; you do not have the report, so now you must hunt down the auditors. What about that report that you e-mailed two months ago that the auditors misplaced? Do you still have it in your sent folder to resend to them? If not, can you find it somewhere on your computer so that you can send it?

All of these situations happen regularly in the course of an audit conducted via e-mail. In the best case, they are time-consuming nuisances. In the worst case, you can be dealing with an inaccurate finding. The best solution to this problem is to create a centralized repository. Whether you use Lotus Notes, eRoom, SharePoint, or simply a shared drive directory, pick a location accessible by all parties involved in the audit. Of course, be sure to secure this location adequately because you will be populating it with sensitive information like user access, IP addresses, risk assessment results, and the like—not things you want anyone in the company to be able to access. Also, be sure that each of your external auditors obtains his or her user ID and password to access this repository.

Once you have picked a location and know who needs access, set up the directory structure and any additional access controls you may want. For example, you may group your evidence by control (e.g., approvals, terminations, monitoring, hardening, etc.) or you may group your documentation by type (processes, reports, etc.). You may wish to make read-only folders containing internal documentation for your external auditors and read-only folders containing audit results for your internal personnel.

Depending on the size of your company and therefore the magnitude of the audit, the creation of the audit repository may be fairly straightforward or it may take a few design sessions. The goal of this exercise is to come up with a directory structure that is intuitive and easily used by everyone so that there is consistency in posting information and anyone new to the audit process can easily navigate the structure and find the information he or she seeks. This setup should be a one-time process; if you do it right, you should be able to use your directory structure for years to come, with only minor modifications as the scope of the audit evolves. Therefore, put some thought into it up front and involve all interested parties for their input. It may still be a slightly iterative process requiring some modifications after an audit has ended and additional lessons have been learned, but this repository can help you avoid a lot of headaches in the area of communications.

Step 3—Document, Document, Document

It is not unusual for the personnel on your audit team to change in the course of a single audit. Consider yourself lucky if your audit team does not experience any changes within the year. If you experience continuity of audit personnel across two or more years, you should be ecstatic! The reality is that the audit industry experiences fairly high turnover. Also, because audit firms have so many clients, even if the same people are still employed at the firm, it is difficult to time their staffing to coincide with the same clients' audits each year. The companies being audited bear the brunt of this because they must explain their processes ad nauseum to each new person that walks through the door.

In all fairness to the auditors, most of their employees are well qualified to conduct an audit—theoretically. But the reality is that each company's application of each common audit control is different. Each company runs on different platforms, has different legacy and home-grown applications, and manages its operations differently. Thus, irrespective of how qualified and experienced your external auditors are, you will still need to explain thoroughly how things work in your particular situation, and that explanation is crucial. If the auditors misunderstand or you omit a key bit of information, the subsequent testing may be incorrect or inappropriate, leading to findings that do not actually apply. This, in turn, leads to rework—"re-re-explaining" your processes, providing new evidence, having the auditors retest, and so on. The resource drain can be substantial on all sides.

From a cost–management perspective, the goal of making your audit processes operational is to be more efficient. From an audit and image perspective, the goal is to get accurate results. If you are truly lacking something, then it should show up on the auditor's report, and you should fix it. If you are doing the right thing already, the auditors should understand that and give you credit for it. But in an ad hoc environment, it is woefully easy to omit providing a key piece of evidence, or for the auditor to misinterpret that evidence, or for an explanation to leave with someone that has left the team.

The primary solution to this problem is to document *everything* and post it to your newly created repository. This strategy may not sound cost effective at first, but in the long run you will realize significant savings and value by expending fewer resources during audits and establishing consistent standards that are reusable over time. Here is a list of the things that should be made available to the auditors:

- Process documents. Document each process that your company executes for each control. Develop a standardized process document format that will be used by everyone to ensure that all relevant information is captured and that the documentation is clear to everyone. Be sure to be thorough—remember that your primary audience will be individuals from the outside who will not be familiar with your internal personnel, systems, or acronyms. Err on the side of caution and explain everything. You should also have a process for creating new processes (identifying when they are needed) and updating existing processes (how to do that efficiently, who needs to review, how to identify when a change is needed, etc.).

- Legend for each report created. As much as possible, you should standardize your reports so that they are familiar to everyone. This will help your operations personnel as well as your auditors because if they must do any remediation or other cleanup they can receive a number of reports that look the same, which will make it easier for them to address the findings accurately. However, no matter how much you standardize the reports within a control, you will still have a variety of reports across controls with naturally different content. The column headings and contents of the reports may still be confusing for someone coming from outside the organization. Therefore, document the contents of each report type: explain what information is found in each column, and what (if anything) can be inferred from that information.

  Also explain what the lack of information means in your report. If a field is left blank, does that mean that information was not available or that it was not obtained? The legend should also clearly state the frequency of report generation. If an auditor thinks you run a particular report weekly but you actually run it monthly, the auditor will document that you are not keeping up with your control. The goal of the legend is to be sufficiently explanatory so that people needing to review the report in question can simply refer to the legend and understand what they are viewing and how often they should expect to see another version. They should not have to take the time of someone in your organization to walk them through how to decipher the report or tell them how many reports are available for the past year. Of course, they may still have specific content questions that cannot be covered in the legend, but that will consume a much smaller portion of your team's time.

■ Reports as audit artifacts. As you are documenting your processes, standardizing your reports, and creating your legends, you should consider whether you are producing adequate reports. One of the key ways that companies "fail" an audit is by being unable to produce evidence. They may have a perfectly adequate process for maintaining control, but if that process is not documented and reports are not generated to demonstrate that the process is working, the auditors will have no choice but to log a finding. Therefore, for each control, ask, "Can I prove that I am doing this?" If the answer is "no," fix that now because in many cases it is difficult or impossible to generate reports retroactively.

■ Tracking metrics. Part of the audit consists of the auditors gaining "comfort" that your processes are working. They gain this comfort by seeing evidence that you are executing your processes on an ongoing basis throughout the year and not simply scrambling in the month or two before their arrival. When you create tracking metrics such as checklists and perpetual calendars, showing when certain tasks were supposed to get done, what actions were taken if something did not get done on time, and that the tasks are generally completed in a timely fashion, the auditors will gain tremendous comfort that your processes are working.

■ Meeting minutes. Create a standard meeting minutes template (if your company does not already have one that works for you) and enforce its use. Be sure that someone documents each audit meeting that occurs and post the minutes to the repository. If there are follow-up action items or issues, keep an action-item or issues log and track these to completion. Auditors always want to know who did what, so make sure that on all of the minutes and logs there is a space to indicate the full name of the person who created the minutes, the individual responsible for resolving an issue, or the person who completed the action item. Titles should also be included, especially if the person is associated with a verification or approval.

■ Frequently asked questions (FAQs). Over time, you may discover that other explanations that did not fit neatly into your process documents or report legends are needed. For these, create and post an FAQ document. In this case, frequent means more than once. If someone asks you a question, chances are someone else in the future will ask the same question. This can be as a result of turnover or lack of communication within other teams. To avoid answering the same question multiple times (and perhaps having different people interpret the answer differently or different people provide the answer in conflicting ways), set the rule that anyone with a question should document it in the FAQ section in your audit repository. The answer should be provided in the same place by the person most qualified to give an answer. The answer should be as complete as possible, providing any needed background information to set the context.

Clearly, getting all of your documentation together can be a fairly large undertaking. However, this is also a one-time activity. Once it is established, it will be relatively easy to maintain the documentation, and you only need to get the people who provide reports to provide them on time. But by having all of your processes clearly documented and posted in a well-organized and easily navigated central repository, you can set the expectation with your auditors that their activities should be largely self-service. If they bring someone new to the team, that person should review all of the posted process documents and FAQs first and then discuss any questions with teammates, contacting your team only if the first two options have been exhausted. If the new team member does have questions for your people, they and the corresponding answers are documented so the next new person does not need to ask.

You can take this a step further by providing enough reports for the auditors to be able to select their samples and then find the evidence without engaging your team. For example, in the area of access controls, the auditors will look at terminations. It is very important that users who have left the company no longer have access to certain critical applications. If you post a monthly report of active users on your critical applications, as well as a monthly list of terminated users from your Human Resource (HR) system, the auditors can select a sample of users from the HR report, select a sample of critical applications that they wish to verify, and then review the monthly user reports from those applications to determine whether those users still have access.

The alternative is for the auditor to sit with one or more individuals from your company who can log into the respective systems and look up each selected user individually. If you do choose self-service auditing of certain controls as described here, be sure to discuss this with your auditor in advance to determine what level of granularity is required. For example, if the auditor wants to test that a user was terminated within a few days of his or her departure, but you run monthly reports, this may not be adequate. You will also need to determine whether creating a sufficient number of reports to make auditing self-service is more cost effective or time consuming than having the auditors sit with someone. This will largely depend on the size of your user base and the number of critical applications that fall into the scope of your audits.

Anatomy of a Process Document

Many companies do not have a standard process template that they use, or it is inadequate for the purposes of depicting a control process. This section provides guidelines on how to create a process template that can be widely and effectively used.

A process document has three main sections: the introduction, the actual process flow diagram, and a description of each step in the flow. The introductory section should contain the following information:

- Purpose and scope. What is the purpose of this process? How and when will it be used? By whom? In what capacity?
- Assumptions. Many processes have certain prerequisites or conditions that must be met for them to be effective. For example, you may need to assume that certain personnel are available, that specific people have the privileges to execute a task, or that a particular system is available.
- Definition of terms. Be sure to define all acronyms or internal terms used in your process, especially if you abbreviate any team or system names so that they fit in your process diagram. The list of terms should not be enormous; within any given process, there should not be more than a handful of terms to define.

If you find that a lot of terms need definition and are repeated across processes fairly frequently, you may wish to consider creating a master glossary. Reference that in each of your process documents.

■ Ownership and approval. Who owns maintaining this process? Who owns executing the process? If changes are made to the process, who is responsible for reviewing and approving the changes? Ownership should be defined in terms of titles or teams, not individual names.

■ Customer. Who is the customer of this process (i.e., who benefits from its execution)? As with owners, customers should be defined in terms of titles or teams, not individual names.

■ Inputs and entry criteria. What initiates this process? What components are needed to activate the process? These are two different questions. For example, if you are documenting an access control process, the process may be initiated by a user submitting an access request, but if the request is incomplete or the user has not provided required supporting documentation, the process cannot continue. It is important to document all of the components needed to execute the process end to end.

■ Outputs and exit criteria. What are the deliverables of this process? How do you know that the process has been executed to completion? In the previous access request example, the process would be completed when the user has been approved or denied access. If the access was denied, the sole output would be a documented denial. If the access was approved, the outputs would include a documented approval, confirmation from the access administrator that access was granted, and possibly documented proof that the user completed training if that is necessary to use the system.

■ Links to other processes. Some processes are directly or indirectly related to other processes. If that is the case, those other processes should be referenced by title and location. For consistency across process documents, this entry should always appear. If there are no related processes, this should be indicated.

The introduction and assumptions sections will obviously need to be in text format. The terms can be displayed as a bulleted list or a table—whichever you prefer—as long as you maintain consistency across your process documents. The remaining items are best displayed in a table because the information for each item is fairly limited.

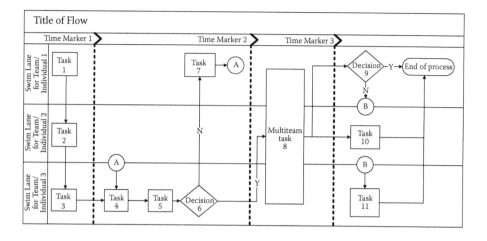

Figure 7.1 Process flow template. This depicts the appropriate setup of a process flow diagram, including use of swim lanes to denote tasks completed by different individuals or teams, use of time markers (if needed), indication of multiteam tasks, alignment of shapes vertically and horizontally for readability, consistency of direction in yes and no connectors from decisions, numbering of shapes for referencing in the process flow table shown in table 7.1, and use of reference circles to avoid connectors pointing to the left (reference circles A) or crossing (reference circles B). Swim lane titles should reference team names or titles of individuals, not names of individuals. Time markers may be in any unit (hours, days, weeks), but should be consistent (i.e., time marker 1 should not be denoted in hours if time marker 2 is denoted in days). Sample processes are provided in chapter 12.

The second section of your process document is the process flow—a visual representation of how the process is executed. Different people have different comfort levels with process diagrams. By maintaining consistency across process documents and following the standard rules of flow diagrams, you will increase the overall comfort level of your readers and also ensure that there is no confusion. Refer to figure 7.1 as you read the following bulleted items to get a clear understanding of the contents of the process flow diagram.

■ Delineate actions required by different individuals or teams by using "swim lanes." The lanes should go horizontally across the page and be labeled to the left.
■ If the process is time sensitive, include time markers vertically in the appropriate places.

- Indicate actions with a box. The box should be in the swim lane of the group or person who executes that task. If the task is performed simultaneously by two or more groups, size the box to cover all applicable swim lanes (this may affect the order in which you list the teams in the swim lanes).
- Indicate questions (decision points) with a diamond.
- Determine a standard for the "yes" and "no" connectors coming from a decision point. Typically, "yes" is to the right and "no" is from the top or bottom. You could have it the other way around, as long as it is consistent within the process documents.
- Connectors should only point to the right, upward, or downward—never to the left. If you need to create a loop, use the circle as a reference. Attach the connector to the circle and label the circle with the first available letter (A, B, C, etc.). At the point where you want to begin the loop, place another circle with the same letter label and connect it into the next task or decision (this is demonstrated in figure 7.1 by the circle references labeled with the letter A).
- Connectors should not cross each other. To avoid crossing connectors, use the circle reference similar to the way it is described above. (This is demonstrated in figure 7.1 by the circle references labeled with the letter B.)
- Use the oval shape to indicate the end of a process.
- Use the pentagon shape to indicate that the next step is the initiation of another process.
- All shapes in the process, except for the circle references and the oval end-of-process, should be numbered. The process steps should be numbered roughly in the order in which they occur, with the understanding that the numbering will change slightly when there is a decision point. At decision points, number consistently (e.g., yes first, then no, or vice versa).
- For clarity and readability, align shapes vertically and horizontally.

The third section of the process document is a table that describes each numbered shape in detail. Refer to table 7.1 while reading the following bulleted items describing the contents of that table:

- Column 1, "Step No.," corresponds to the number that was inserted into each shape in the diagram.
- Column 2, "Description," contains the title of the corresponding shape as it appears in the flow diagram. This column also contains

Table 7.1   Process Description Table Template

Step No.	Description	Responsibility	Deliverables
1.	Task 1 Title (as it appears in the flow chart) Steps required to complete task 1 Documentation or other requirements for task 1 Note: Notes for task 1 (e.g., "Task 1 must be completed within one day of submission.")	Title(s) of individual(s) or name(s) of team(s) responsible for completing task 1	List of documents produced in task 1 (e.g., meeting minutes, updated logs, etc.)
2.	Decision 2 Title (as it appears in the flow chart) Define the criteria for deciding yes or no If the decision is yes, proceed to step #x If the decision is no, proceed to step #y.	Title(s) of individual(s) or name(s) of team(s) responsible for making decision 2	It is possible that a decision will not have any deliverables associated with it; in that case, state "none" here; if the decision is documented, indicate the name of the document

a bulleted list of steps involved in the particular task. For example, if the task is "requestor submits a request," the detail may describe what tool is used to submit the request, what needs to be filled out in the request, and what supporting documentation must be attached to the request. There may also be some notes below the bulleted list. For example, you may have a note stating, "If the requestor submits the request after 3 P.M. EST, it will not be reviewed until the following business morning."

■ Column 3, "Responsibility," contains the title of the individual or name of the team responsible for the action. For example, if the task is "requestor submits a request," the responsible party is the requestor. If the task is "grant UNIX access," the responsible party might be "UNIX access administrator" or "UNIX operations team."

■ Column 4, "Deliverables," contains a bulleted list of deliverables generated as a result of the completion of that particular task. For example, in the "requestor submits a request" task, the deliverables would be a completed request and the supporting documentation. If the task is to "conduct review meeting," the deliverables would be the meeting minutes and updated action items and issue logs. Some items may not have a deliverable. If that is the case, indicate "none."

This table will describe in detail each of the shapes in a flow diagram, except for reference circles or end-of-process ovals. The "Step No." column indicates the number of the task or decision shape in the process flow diagram (see figure 7.1). The "Description" column provides the task or decision title as it appears in the process flow diagram, followed by a bulleted list of steps or other information pertaining to the completion of that task or decision. The "Responsibility" column provides the names of the individuals or teams responsible for completing the task or making the decision. The "Deliverables" column provides a list of deliverables (such as meeting minutes, documents, updated logs, etc.) created as a result of executing that task or decision. If no deliverables are created, specify "none." Sample processes are provided in chapter 12.

Of course, at the end of the process document there should be a revision log with the following information:

■ Version modified
■ Name of person that made the modifications
■ Brief description of the modifications made

Winning "Comfort" Points

In this chapter, a number of efficiency techniques have been discussed. Conveniently, things that make an audit more efficient also tend to give auditors more comfort. To summarize, they are:

■ Clearly documenting control processes
■ Creating legends for reports
■ Creating standardized reports
■ Using tracking metrics such as perpetual calendars to demonstrate that the processes are being executed in a timely fashion
■ Developing and documenting an interaction process with other teams and the auditors to make the best use of everyone's time

As previously mentioned, being organized and efficient will save you time and hopefully avoid confusion. It may also improve your chances of passing an audit by helping you identify where you are lacking evidence. But it will not otherwise make you more compliant. If you have some legitimate gaps, they will need to be addressed. This section provides a few more suggestions on how to prepare for an audit.

Align with Policy

It used to be that the accepted practice with security policies was to document how things should be, not how they are, with the goal of achieving the more secure state over time. Documenting a policy that reflects the current state was considered unacceptable because that invariably left weaknesses in the policy.

With the advent of auditing, this mentality has shifted somewhat. Auditors first review a company's policies and then perform their audit against the contents of those policies. They also comment on the policies. This leaves most companies "between a rock and a hard place." If the policy reflects what exists and that is weak, the auditors will find that the company's policies are inadequate. If the policy reflects what should be and the company has not yet achieved that level of security, the auditors will find that the company is not in compliance with its policies.

There is no good solution to this problem. What seems to work for a lot of companies is to modify their policy review cycle to time it against the audit cycle. Companies now review and update their policies near the end of the year, once they have some idea of what the audit findings will be. The new, stronger policies are made available near the first of the year to give responsible parties as much time as possible to remediate their systems and processes before the auditors come back.

Other Considerations

To help the auditors gain comfort that you are doing the right things:

■ Do not leave any blanks in your reports. If information is not available, write in "N/A" or "none." If an answer is needed (e.g., yes or no), make sure that each line item has an answer associated with it. Do not give the auditors the opportunity to question whether a blank cell means "no" or "not verified."

- When possible, save originals. For example, if you obtain validation or approval for certain things via e-mail, it is better to be able to provide the original e-mail rather than copying and pasting the contents into a document of some sort. Depending on your e-mail system, e-mails could be a bit tricky to store. Be sure you have a strategy on how to store such e-mails if they cannot be deposited into your audit repository with everything else. The same applies to hardcopy documents. If you obtain physical signatures for anything, it is best to produce the original document with the actual signature, not copies. Better yet, figure out a way to go paperless.

- Ensure that the auditors share their findings before publishing them. Hopefully, by creating the repository and clearly documenting all of your processes, you have left no room for misunderstanding but anything is possible. If indeed a piece of evidence was omitted or misinterpreted and that led to an incorrect audit finding, it is better to catch this before the senior executives hear that something is wrong.

- Do not be afraid to push back on the auditors. Verify that the tests they executed make sense and are accurate. If their tests do not appropriately reflect your controls, tell them and make them retest. This is something that should be worked out in the initial expectations meetings. It should be clear to both parties how each control will be tested—but if something goes awry anyway, make sure it is addressed before it becomes a finding.

Chapter 8

Reporting Your Value

Introduction

Executive management relies on relevant, consistent, and comprehensive reporting to get a pulse on your department and to make good tactical and strategic decisions. The pragmatic goal of security reporting is to capture and present useful data in an easily digestible format with the appropriate level of abstraction so that your executives can effortlessly grasp the value that your department brings to the company.

How to Make Reports Relevant

The bane of typical security reporting is that it provides a list of meaningless numbers to management, such as number of SPAM e-mails stopped, number of intrusions detected at the firewalls, number of viruses quarantined at the mail gateway, and so on, without making these numbers relevant to the business. The most important aspect of pragmatic security reporting is to translate security metrics into business terms. To do this, you must understand what is important to your company. If your executive management is focusing on operational efficiencies, then you want to relate significant portions of your security reporting to the appropriate allocation of budget and resources. If they are focusing on productivity, then you want to emphasize the number of security requests that your department has processed or the successful risk mitigation initiatives that you have accomplished.

When determining the appropriate metrics to report, it is also important to understand how benefit realization is viewed in your company to avoid creating reports that could be perceived as making false claims. For example, suppose that the information security department implements a Web security initiative that enables Human Resources (HR) to implement electronic pay stubs, which in turn saves the company $1 million annually in printing and mailing charges. Without the Web security initiative, electronic pay stubs would not even be a consideration. But the existence of Web security does not automatically make electronic pay stubs possible; an additional HR effort was needed. Who gets credit for that million dollar annual savings? Information security? HR? Both?

At a lot of companies, the answer would, unfortunately, be HR only. If that is the case at your company, you need to be aware of that ahead of time and come up with a strategy on how to publicize information security's value when the business is most likely to get the credit for initiatives involving them. Somehow, executive management and the business need to understand that without the efforts of the information security department, a particular business realization would not have been possible.

How to Make Reports Consistent

To produce consistent reports, automate wherever possible. Automation not only saves time that your resources would otherwise spend to collect the data, but it also provides greater accuracy and consistency to your reporting. Once you determine the areas on which you want to report, spend the extra time on the front end to design and automate the collection and compilation of your data. The up-front cost spent on a good design toward automation will reap great benefits down the line when you must produce your weekly, monthly, or quarterly reports.

How to Make Reports Comprehensible

An easily comprehensible security report has useful security information presented in business terms at the right level of detail. Using the guidelines set forth in the previous section titled "How to Make Reports Relevant," identify areas on which you ought to report. Consider the following items:

- Report the status of your major security initiatives and make them relevant to the business by incorporating budget and resource considerations. Use standard red–amber–green (RAG) color coding to indicate the overall "health" of the project.
- Report the status of your security assessment activities (see chapter 2), including outstanding risks and remediation efforts, to illustrate security posture improvements due to completed risk mitigation tasks. This area can produce some impressive metrics, especially in large organizations where findings or devices can number in the hundreds or thousands. Statements such as "successfully hardened 500 of 600 servers" or "reduced the number of exceptions from 1,357 to 498" make a very good impression.
- Report on the number of security reviews conducted and include notes about tangible benefits to the business because of the review, such as operational efficiency, standardization, potential cost savings, etc.
- Report on security incidents and include facts relevant to the business, such as cost of the incident, hours of downtime, approximate savings due to quick resolution, and status on mitigating the risk exposure. Better yet, if recently implemented security processes or technologies stopped an incident from occurring, be sure to highlight that.
- Report on compliance activities by defining the number of authorizations processed, exceptions granted, new administrative processes defined, and audits conducted. Make it relevant to the business by connecting compliance activities with the goal of meeting requirements set by regulatory, privacy, and external or internal auditors. It is also useful to highlight areas of improvement in the compliance process based on the trend of authorizations or exceptions processed—for example, policies that need to be revisited due to their interference with certain business processes, resulting in a high number of exceptions granted. Good metrics tracking in the area of compliance will especially help in demonstrating value over time in two ways:
  1. The first way is in the number of hours spent on compliance activities. In chapter 7, we discussed how to operationalize the audit process to reduce substantially the number of man-hours devoted to the annual audit. It is not unusual for large companies to spend hundreds or thousands of man-hours gathering evidence, responding to findings, and so on. If yours is one of those companies, track this and get a baseline. As you make your audit processes operational, you will be

able to show a significant decrease in the number of man-hours needed to execute an audit.

2. Second, capture the number of findings, exceptions, or violations that are found. It is expected that an initial audit or assessment will result in a fairly large number of findings. However, as you work on remediation and improve your processes to better maintain your more secure state, the number of findings will drop precipitously. Be sure to baseline the number of findings up front so that you can demonstrate how dramatically that number drops over time.

■ Report on security awareness initiatives to illustrate the different target audiences that are reached with what message during what period. Make it relevant to the business by demonstrating how the awareness campaigns have improved compliance or resulted in fewer incidents.

Section 4

SECURITY TECHNOLOGIES— ESTABLISHING A SOUND FOUNDATION

In the current digital age, businesses and consumers depend heavily on data networks. These business systems are susceptible to attacks from basically anywhere in the world by someone with an Internet connection. Add to that fact the rising threat of identity theft and sophisticated automated attacks (viruses and bots) and you have a formula for trouble. Throw in increased regulatory requirements, Wall Street expectations (for public companies), and budgetary concerns for an underfunded and unprepared security program and you have a recipe for disaster.

This section helps you construct levees to weather the volatile climate of today's security threats. You will also see how three out of the six departmental goals outlined in chapter 1 are met by having a strong strategy for security technologies. Those goals are:

- Help the business meet its objectives in a secure, cost-effective, and efficient way.
- Ensure minimal downtime to business critical functions due to security incidents.
- Ensure minimal compromise to confidential data due to security incidents.

We will also connect to the discussion in chapter 3 about the roles of security architects and engineers by exemplifying their responsibilities in assessing, reviewing, and architecting security solutions that reduce risks for the company. The objective of security engineers and architects is to develop innovative security components that can be made operational or automated. Establishing the right security infrastructure up front reduces the cost of security operations, eliminates the need to reverse-engineer deficient technologies in production, and minimizes the risk of security incidents.

There are three chapters in this section. Chapter 9, "Risk Assessment," discusses a pragmatic methodology to conduct annual security assessments to identify and remediate high-risk areas. Chapter 10, "Security Design Review," focuses on the regular analysis of risk in new and ongoing IT or business initiatives. Chapter 11, "Exploit Protection," describes a cost-effective approach to managing threats and vulnerabilities, to reduce the likelihood of security incidents that threaten business uptime and the compromise of information assets.

Chapter 9

Risk Assessment

Introduction: The Truth about Risk Assessments

Most of us have paid for or participated in hiring outside vendors or consultants to conduct risk assessments of our enterprise. They run their tools, conduct interviews, and produce a final deliverable that reads like scare-tactic propaganda with a list of remediation items (that they would gladly help you remediate for a nominal fee). The remediation items tend to be constructed out of some industry best-practice template and typically do not consider the technological constraints of your environment, the political climate needed to get the right momentum, and the budget needed to accomplish the recommended mitigation initiatives. Returning to a key point in chapter 1: Industry best practices may not always be practical for your environment. These security assessments can cost tens of thousands of dollars, tie up valuable resources, take up valuable time, and send you down the impractical path of addressing risks according to best practices as opposed to dealing with threats that can cripple your environment.

There is a time and place for external assessments. If you are an IT service provider, getting an external assessment of security such as SAS-70 or SysTrust may be an efficient way to prove your security posture to prospective clients. You may also engage an external third party to fulfill an audit requirement specific to your industry. If you are strapped for time or resources, augmenting your staff with qualified consultants to fill an immediate need is not a bad thing to do.

In fact, you may benefit from their speed and focus. Although the best-practices methodologies that they bring with them may not be quite right for your practical situation, their experience with many other companies will likely enable them to obtain information more expediently, and they may be able to provide guidance on perplexing situations if they have seen how their other clients have resolved similar problems. The thing to note here is that any external assessment that is performed must be "sanity checked" by internal resources in the context of legacy systems and politics to ensure that the results are meaningful and not misleading.

But before spending a lot of time and effort looking at every last detail of every last system in your company, first take a step back and look at your risks from the enterprise level. You would be surprised at how easy it is to assemble a list of risks that could severely cripple your enterprise. As a matter of fact, you probably know a lot of them off the top of your head. To add to that list, walk down to the managers of different key business and IT operations. They could probably ramble off a list of high-priority risks that they are aware of in their operations.

The truth is that if you create a safe atmosphere for them to disclose those risks to you, they would. Communicate to them that if they do not tell you, they must assume full responsibility of those risks if they are exploited. By bringing these risks to light, you could escalate them to executive management, prioritize them accordingly, and collaborate with these managers to remediate the risks in a reasonable time frame. In the remainder of this chapter, we formulate the strategic and tactical goals for establishing an effective internal security assessment program.

Strategy for Conducting Annual Internal Risk Assessments

With the advent of Sarbanes–Oxley (SOX) and other regulatory audits, annual risk assessments on at least your critical systems are now mandatory. You must conduct these assessments annually, they must be a little bit more thorough each year, and you must address the findings. If you do not have an organized and efficient methodology for executing these assessments, you could be spending a lot more time on these assessments than is needed and miss some key vulnerabilities. You should therefore strive to establish an annual internal security assessment program that becomes part of your IT and business culture. The assessment should have an annual life cycle as depicted in table 9.1.

Because risk assessments are such a critical component of the annual audit, the risk assessment life cycle is positioned to coincide

Table 9.1 Suggested Annual Life Cycle for Conducting Risk Assessments

Time Frame	Key Activities
This year: Q3–Q4	Identify key areas to assess, based on the business determination of which are the company's critical systems Plan for the security assessment Conduct the assessment Consolidate the findings Package findings for delivery to executives and managers
This year: Q4	Prioritize findings based on risk criteria Provide summary of risk to executive management Reprioritize findings according to executive management's risk appetite Socialize remediation efforts Embed remediation efforts into the following year's objectives and budget
Next year: Q1–Q2	Execute remediation activities Negotiate exceptions and determine compensating controls Provide risk status reports to executive management
Next year: Q3–Q4	Plan for the security assessment Incorporate leftover findings from last year Conduct the assessment Consolidate the findings Package findings for delivery to executives and managers

with the audit cycle. That is, assessments must be conducted in the latter half of the year so that responsible parties have the first half of the following year to execute remediations or implement compensating controls in time for the next audit cycle.

The battle lies in getting this type of assessment program off the ground. Engage your corporate sponsors, talk to your peers, and effectively articulate the value of such a program by stressing the following points:

■ It costs less and can be done more quickly than external security assessments.
■ It provides a more accurate picture of risk due to the intrinsic understanding of internal IT and business environment.

- It creates consistency and efficiency by establishing an annual process, which also gives "comfort" to the auditors (more about this in section 3).
- It establishes a measurable improvement of security posture over time.

Once this cycle becomes a part of your corporate culture, you will have a cost-effective process to identify, prioritize, and remediate high-risk areas in your organization. However, it is important to note that the internal security assessment does not necessarily take the place of an external security review. Some companies, such as those that must conform to the payment card industry's data security standard, may be subjected to external reviews after a reported security intrusion. There is also value in scheduling an objective third-party review of your security posture every other year. The external review provides an unbiased view of your security to external auditors or customers. Additionally, external reviewers may uncover risk areas that you may have missed due to overfamiliarity with your environments.

Tactical Perspective for Security Assessment

Tactically, your security assessment should aim to achieve the following:

- Appropriate scope: The assessment should cover key risk areas across the entire enterprise and avoid unimportant areas.
- Organized methodology: The assessment should be executed in an organized way to avoid omissions or rework.
- Speed: The assessment should take no longer than one quarter to complete for a smaller company or two quarters for a larger company.

These concepts are briefly discussed in the following subsections.

Appropriate Scope

The goal of your security assessment coverage is to ensure that you have determined the threats and vulnerabilities that can severely exploit your key business functions and can exclude those risks that would be time consuming to mitigate and do not provide significant value in increasing your overall security posture. Table 9.2 presents the minimum set of questions you should consider when defining your scope and suggests some actions to take with respect to each question.

Table 9.2   Questions and Corresponding Actions When Building a Risk Assessment Process

Questions	Actions
What are your company's key business functions?	Make a list of the key business functions and determine the systems that support that function. This activity should be performed in conjunction with key business stakeholders to ensure that the list of key functions accurately reflects the business view, not the IT or information security view.
Who manages these systems?	Make a list of business executives and IT managers with whom you will need to speak.
How resistant do you think IT and business management will be toward your assessment activities?	Strategize around the executive buyoff you will need to mobilize your security assessment. This is the most difficult in the first year when you are trying to establish the assessment life cycle and embed it into the company's culture.
What areas are noncritical and can be eliminated or postponed?	Do not try to cover every system in your enterprise. Focus on systems critical to the business. Talk to key business executives and managers to understand what they cannot live without for a day.
Who on your team can conduct security assessments?	Assemble a special team within your department to conduct these assessments. It would be ideal if you could utilize every member for this initiative.

By asking and answering these questions, you can more accurately set the scope of your assessments and also anticipate potential stumbling blocks and come up with a plan for addressing them before they exert an impact on your timeline.

Organized Methodology

It is very important to make the assessment logical and intuitive for those executing the assessments or receiving the results. Do not convolute the process with unnecessary tools, processes, or paperwork; and be sure to develop with an organized methodology to avoid omitting steps and having to go back and complete them. Table 9.3 presents a road map to assist you in getting your assessment done in an organized fashion.

Table 9.3   Phased Sequence of Events in Conducting a Risk Assessment

Phase	Activities	Deliverables
Planning	Determine areas that you want to cover. At a minimum, you should cover three areas: key IT infrastructure systems, key business applications, and end-user computing. Assemble your team of interviewers. Form your interviewee list. Create a task list or project plan to cover areas and align interviewers with interviewees. Compile the tools needed to conduct assessment.	Assessment team staffing (interviewers) List of interviewees Task list or project plan Compiled assessment tools
Positioning	Prepare a value proposition promoting the benefits of the security assessment. Hold meetings with, send e-mails, and talk to the relevant executives and managers to get their support to push this assessment through.	Value proposition statement
Interviewing	Form two sets of questions: common questions to ask every group and specific questions customized to the area being assessed. To expedite the interview process, send the interviewees a copy of the questions you will ask them ahead of time and give them a chance to review and respond. If they have any questions, set up a face-to-face meeting, but many of your interviewees will be able to provide their answers offline via e-mail. As the assessments come in, start capturing the likelihood of the risk, degree of damage, and potential remediation activities.	Security assessment questionnaire Detailed findings

Table 9.3 (Continued)   Phased Sequence of Events in Conducting a Risk Assessment

Phase	Activities	Deliverables
Validation	Use the selected security assessment tools to validate specific areas on an as-needed basis, based on the results of the interviews. Over time, as the obvious vulnerabilities are remediated, the tools will play an increasingly large role in identifying the smaller or more obscure vulnerabilities. Perform a sanity check of the tool findings against the realities of your infrastructure. Although vulnerability scanning tools are fairly mature, they still sometimes provide false-positive results. Ask to review system or application logs or documentation relevant to your assessment.	Reports from assessment tools Analysis of logs and documentation reviewed
Prioritization	Gather your assessment team along with other subject-matter experts and stakeholders to review the detailed findings. Evaluate the likelihood of each risk, weighed against the damage it could cause. Discuss possible resolutions and the costs to fix. Keep an eye out for opportunities to increase operational efficiencies or cut costs. Create a findings matrix that summarizes all the detailed findings. Assign owners to each finding in the findings matrix and follow up with them on whether they agree with the remediation activities. Edit the detailed findings and findings matrix according to discussions with the owners.	Findings matrix Remediation plan

(*continued*)

Table 9.3 (Continued)   Phased Sequence of Events in Conducting a Risk Assessment

Phase	Activities	Deliverables
	Once all the responses on the findings have come in, start developing a remediation plan to address the high-risk areas.	
Presentation	Once you have finalized the findings matrix, plot the findings on a risk chart that has likelihood on the x-axis, cost to fix on the y-axis, and colors to signify degree of damage (red = high, yellow = medium, green = low). Prepare an executive summary that highlights the key areas of the assessment, such as the top ten risks, the risk chart, and the remediation plan.	Risk chart (see figure 9.1) Executive summary of security assessment
Remediation	Execute the remediation plan. Update the findings matrix as issues are closed.	Updated findings matrix
Wrap-up	Present finalized findings matrix to appropriate parties. Get necessary sign-off validating that risks have been remediated.	Finalized findings matrix

Activities and deliverables are outlined by phase, beginning with planning, then obtaining support from executive management, executing the assessment, validating the findings, determining a course of remediation, and publicizing the results. Figure 9.1 presents an example of the risk chart discussed in the "presentation" row of table 9.3.

Speed

Nothing is more ineffective than a convoluted process that does not seem to produce results in a timely manner. Furthermore, your ability to pass the next audit may depend on your quick execution of the next risk assessment, allowing time for remediation. Credibility is often earned by quick follow-through. Table 9.4 outlines an assessment plan for a 10,000-person company.

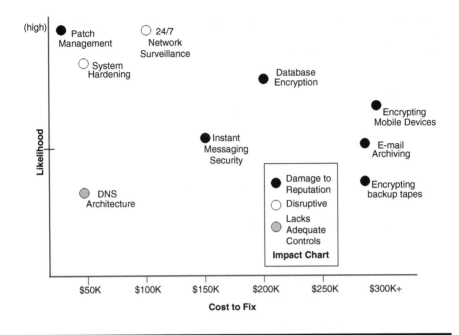

Figure 9.1 Risk chart. This chart is an example of how to map the various risk findings in a two-dimensional figure that reflects cost to fix, likelihood of the risk, and potential impact. Note that this is an example only; the cost to fix will vary by size of the organization and degree of current capability. The impact of certain risks will also vary by industry and current technologies used.

Use table 9.4 as a guideline to form your security assessment project plan. Be sure to adjust the suggested resource quantities, man-hours, and durations according to the size of your organization. Man-hours, resource quantities, and durations assume a medium-sized company with skilled resources. Smaller companies may be able to execute an assessment faster. Larger companies will likely take longer because there are more individuals to interview and a greater number of systems to scan. The values will also change over time within the company as assessment executors and participants become more experienced and efficient and as the number of findings diminishes due to previous years' remediation activities.

Just to be clear, the risk assessment initiative is done amid your normal operational and risk management activities. Assessment should not take up 100 percent of your time. You need to use your resources effectively to conduct the assessment and follow-up on remediation

Table 9.4 Sample Resource Planning Metrics per Assessment Phase for a 10,000-Person Company

Phase	Man-hours	Resource and duration
Planning	Coverage determination: 4 hours Assemble team: 2 hours Form an interviewee list: 2 hours Create a task list: 4 hours Compile tools: 4 hours	One manager One week
Positioning	Value proposition: 4 hours Communication: 16 hours	One manager One week
Interviewing	Prepare questionnaire: 8 hours Conduct interviews: 80 hours Compile findings: 40 hours	Four resources Three weeks
Validation	Run tools: 8 hours Update findings: 8 hours	Two resources Two weeks
Prioritization	Prioritize risk: 16 hours Create findings matrix: 8 hours Communicate findings to owners: 32 hours Create remediation plan: 8 hours	Three resources Two weeks
Presentation	Develop risk chart: 8 hours Develop executive summary: 8 hours	Two resources One week
Remediation	Man-hours will depend on the number and complexity of remediation items	Number of resources to be determined One to two quarters

items as an annual activity. The assessment will help you root out high-priority risks so that you are allocating your limited time and resources to threats and vulnerabilities that can have a severe impact on your business or security program.

Remediation Strategy

From your risk assessment, you will have a list of prioritized risks captured in the "findings matrix." Depending on your pre-existing security posture, this could be a short or a long list. If you are one of the fortunate ones with the short list, move on to the next chapter. If you have a long list of remediations, you need a mechanism for further isolating the most important areas on which to focus. One mechanism is to identify your top ten risks. This list should also help in your efforts to communicate and deliver effectively. Executives are not interested and will not register seeing page after page of risk findings. They will definitely remember the existence of a top-ten risk list and how quickly that list shrinks. Ensure that you provide appropriate accountability as you remediate these risks. The following steps will help you formulate the top ten risks for your enterprise:

Step 1: Put on the filter of "Focus on Your High Risk Areas" (as described in chapter 1) and analyze the security threats that can severely affect your company's business. Consider security breaches that have happened to other companies, especially in your industry. Lost backup tapes, hacking, lost or stolen laptops, and dishonest insiders are recurring themes that result in a significant compromise of confidential data and that make the news. Also, keep a pulse on the different types of popular and highly destructive automated threats that can cripple the availability of your company's core business functions. From your finding matrix, reprioritize your risk based on the frequency of the threats you see in the news. Do you need encryption to guard against stolen or missing backup tapes? Do you have protection at the e-mail gateways to strip off malicious attachments? Do you have proper access control, monitoring, and segregation of duties to prevent insider attacks?

Once you have factored recent security breaches into your findings matrix and reordered your list, isolate the top ten risks and put the rest on layaway. You cannot overcommit to initiatives if you do not have the budget, the personnel, or the time. If you spread yourself too thin, you will end up with mediocre or half-baked defenses that do not live up to their full potential, thus lowering your return on investment (ROI) and compromising your security posture.

Step 2: Consider the pain points in your security program from the previous year. Did you suffer from security incidents due to vulnerabilities in your posture that you have not patched? Now, check your pain points against the top-ten risks list. Are the pain points included? If not, you must determine which risk you would like to swap to keep the maximum number to ten. Keep your top ten risks intact and put the rest in the layaway batch.

Step 3: Factor in your business's strategic and tactical direction. In this step, you are looking to anticipate future risks as well as looking for areas of collaboration. Depending on where your business is going, you need to examine the potential risk areas that you may need to address if they get there. For example, if there is a business initiative to outsource key capabilities offshore, you need to anticipate the risk of confidential data in the hands of third parties. Has that been incorporated in your top-ten risks list? Do the same as in step 2 by demoting and replacing risks to keep the list at ten.

Step 4: Formulate initiatives to address the top ten risks. You do not need to have ten security initiatives to handle ten risks. The idea here is to consolidate your initiatives in such a way that you can eliminate multiple risks with fewer initiatives. For example, an encryption initiative could address the risks of compromised information assets due to stolen backup tapes, hacks against the databases, and missing laptops. Follow the guidelines for high-impact initiatives outlined in chapter 2. Understand that initiatives do equate to buying new security products. Be especially sensitive to security products you already own and whether they are currently living up to their full potential. Did you purchase a suite of products with your license but are only using one or two features of that suite? Do the other paid-for components line up to remediate risks in your top-ten risks list? Talk to your pre-existing vendors about other offerings they may have and negotiate package deals.

There is a flurry of mergers and acquisition activities among the heavyweights in the security product space. The major players are buying up capabilities to provide a total security package to their customers. See whether you can leverage your current vendor relationship to knock out some of your top ten risks without breaking the bank. On a similar front, talk to your IT managers and find areas of collaboration. Are they doing any projects that may cut down on your top ten risks? Is there an opportunity to join forces to meet IT and security needs and split the cost? Be creative and think outside the box on formulating your exploit protection initiatives. Attach a ballpark price tag to each project and reprioritize accordingly.

Step 5: Get the green light and deliver. Follow your company's process of getting the appropriate traction and funding behind your mitigation initiatives and focus on execution. While you are in the process of shoring up your risk areas, be sure to have your incident response team primed to address any potential exploit that may strike at any time (see chapter 13).

Step 6: Do not forget the less critical risks (those we previously termed "layaways"). You can address the layaways opportunistically as other IT or business initiatives may create the requirement, funding, or backing for you to address these risks. Another way of addressing risks not in the top ten is to delegate remediation activities to other relevant IT or business groups. Get appropriate management to accept responsibilities for the risks found, pass the ownership of remediation to them, track them on a periodic basis, and provide remediation status to executive management. This allows you to promote remediation activities without committing significant resources to the effort.

Chapter 10

Security Design Review

Introduction

Projects are constantly developed and initiated to improve or implement new business functions. A majority of these initiatives probably have an IT component and process confidential or business-critical information. While you are mitigating risks in various areas, these projects are opening new avenues for vulnerabilities. To maintain a sustainable security posture throughout your enterprise, you need to review the security component of these projects prior to their deployment. Projects that do not go through security reviews may have the following implications:

- A higher risk of exposure of information assets due to weak security can result in regulatory penalties, legal liabilities, and loss of reputation.
- The lack of security in one implementation may lead to an exposure that can indirectly affect the entire company's security posture and disrupt the ability to do business (a virus or worm attack).
- The lack of security controls on projects that are deployed can lead to negative audit findings.
- Postimplementation corrective measures to address security issues can be disruptive to the business, expensive to fix (resources and time), and difficult to implement (reverse-engineer security back into an insecure system).

The security design review (SDR) process is a mechanism to alleviate these issues by inserting security controls throughout a project's life cycle. For the purposes of this chapter, we will segregate a project life cycle into the following phases:

- Analysis: In this phase, the business analyzes whether the project is worth funding. Project objectives, high-level requirements, and ballpark costs are gathered to present a business case to decision makers.
- Requirements: This is the phase in which the project is funded and detailed requirement gathering begins.
- Design: During this phase requirements are mapped to a design. Prototyping also falls into this phase.
- Build and test: This is the phase in which hardware and software are procured and built or developed. The pilot is typically done now. A range of testing ensues, such as unit testing, integration testing, user acceptance testing, performance testing, and product testing.
- Deploy: In this phase the project goes into production.
- Postproduction: The project goes into maintenance mode in this phase.

The goals of the SDR are to:

- Enable the business to function securely
- Establish a set of security requirements for the project
- Provide security subject matter expertise during the design phase
- Verify that security requirements are met in the build and test phases
- Address security remediations or grant exceptions before the final rollout
- Ensure that the security posture is upheld in the maintenance phase

The Analysis Phase

At this time, the project does not really exist so there are no tangible risks. Your concern here should be to ensure that the project manager captures some high-level security requirements, sets realistic timelines, and allocates an appropriate budget toward security activities. Depending on the security implications of the project, you also may want to provide a preliminary risk assessment so that the executives understand what they are getting into. Do not spend too much time and energy in this phase because many projects die on the vine during the funding process.

Focus your security resources elsewhere but keep an ear open for the outcome of the business case for the project.

The Requirements Phase

In this phase, the project has been funded and work begins. The SDR team's role is to work with the project manager to set the appropriate requirements to meet business, corporate, regulatory, and legal requirements. Ensure that these requirements are captured in the project's requirements document.

Define Information Protection Requirements

If your company has a data classification policy or standard, this portion of the review will be easy. Identify the type or types of data that the project has and apply your data classification requirements. If your company does not have a data classification policy or standard, you can still follow along by classifying your data within the following data types:

- Public data: information available to the general public and intended for distribution outside the organization:
    - Require that the project engage your company's public relations or corporate communications department to review and approve all data for public consumption.
    - Require that data on public Web sites be secured from tampering and defacement.
- Internal use data: information used for intracompany communications but with few or no consequences if compromised:
    - Require that the data not be made available outside the company.
- Confidential data: customer and business information that if inadvertently disclosed could have an adverse impact on the organization, customers, employees, and business partners:
    - Require that data transmitted over public lines (Internet) be encrypted.
    - Require that data be stored in the appropriate network segment for confidential data.
    - Require that data reside on hardened servers.
    - Require that servers that store confidential data be backed up regularly (restore procedures should be in place as well).
    - Require that access to confidential data have an appropriate audit trail.

- Restricted: information categorized as the most sensitive and intended strictly for limited use by authorized parties (e.g., corporate financial data that provides "insider" information); apply all requirements for confidential data to restricted data and add the following:
  - Require that all communications be encrypted.
  - Require that the activities, not the content, around restricted data be monitored and logged.

Define Identity and Access Management Requirements

The majority of your systems have end-user and administrator components. The SDR needs to establish rules around how users are authenticated, authorized, provisioned, changed, disabled, and removed.

- Define your authentication requirements:
  - Define authentication controls such as password complexity, password expiration, password lockout, etc. These should be in line with your password policy or standards.
  - For more sensitive data, you may want to require two-factor authentication through the use of token devices, smart cards, or biometrics.
  - Define requirements around authentication architecture such as integration into a pre-existing user directory.
- Determine the authorization scheme (who has what rights):
  - Define role-based access or rule-based authorizations (see chapter 12 for more details).
  - Require that authorization exercise the "least privilege" principle, whereby users do not have more rights than what they need to do their jobs.
- Consider user-provisioning requirements.
- Consider user-support requirements. This is especially critical because the project or business unit that will use the new system may need to provide funding for additional user administration staff if the demand will be large.

Define Technical Control Requirements

When you are establishing technical security requirements:

- Consider placement of architecture in the appropriate network segments.
- Consider all communication points that require encryption.

- Consider high-availability and backup requirements (including disaster recovery).
- Require the application of all hardening standards.
- Require the protection of audit logs from improper tampering or modification.

Outsourcing Requirements

If the project is an outsourcing initiative, you may want to:

- Verify whether the vendor has any security certifications such as SAS-70 (also mentioned in chapter 4). Ask to review them.
- Verify that the vendor has appropriate controls over information assets.
- Ensure that the vendor has appropriate levels of resiliency.
- If possible, incorporate the right to audit into the contract. This gives you leverage to measure the vendor against your security standards.
- Ensure that responsibilities around compromised confidential data are clearly defined in the contract.
- Ensure that responsibilities around security incident handling and response are clearly defined in the contract.

The Design Phase

In the design phase, technical and nontechnical solutions are formulated and decided upon to meet the stated requirements. You deploy your security architects and engineers to collaborate with the project team to ensure that your security requirements are put into the project's design documentation.

Design Secure Network Architecture

Consider the following when designing security around network-related controls:

- There should be appropriate placement of servers in the DMZ (demilitarized zone).
- Appropriate firewall and intrusion-detection or prevention-monitoring decisions need to be made.

- If it is a Web-centric architecture, establish an *n*-tier design in which separate segments (partitioned by firewalls) are required for Web, application and database.
- If it is a client–server architecture, a Web-brokered proxy should be utilized to consolidate client–server traffic behind a single point (as opposed to every client connecting to the server), to ease the burden of updating clients in various locations (update single client instance on the proxy), to provide a central logging point, and to leverage centralized authentication.
- Confirm the encryption technology to be used. Encryption solutions should be in line with your encryption policy or standards and should be the same as, or similar to, the encryption mechanisms already in use within the organization.

Design Secure System Architecture

Establish hardening guidelines to:

- Ensure that only the minimum necessary operating system packages to run the application are installed.
- Ensure that default permissions are locked down at the file and registry levels.
- Ensure that unneeded services are stopped or removed.
- Ensure that servers have up-to-date system and security patches.
- Separate system partition from data.

Incorporate high availability and redundancy into your design:

- Create clusters for high availability.
- Establish and test backup and restore procedures.
- Evaluate the use of a storage area network (SAN) for space, scalability, and resiliency.

Design system auditing and logging capabilities:

- Log user activities locally and centrally so that you have two copies of the log. The local logs can overwrite while the central log is backed up based on your retention policy.
- If there are higher security requirements, such as for data classified as restricted, logging should incorporate the use of WORM (write once, read many) devices.

Design Secure Application Architecture

Application security is typically the public-facing component of the system. The rise of Web-based hacking has made this area of your design review more critical. These guidelines follow good application development practices:

- Integrate authentication mechanisms with a central user repository as opposed to creating separate silos of user stores.
- Validate user input at the browser and server levels.
- Incorporate administrative logging, alerting, and reporting functions into the application.
- Develop fail-safe exception handling methods.
- Never allow hard-coding of IP addresses, usernames, and passwords.
- Never allow Web servers to connect directly to database servers.
- Always use stored procedures to access tables in the databases (as opposed to direct SQL statements).

The Build and Test Phases

Unless you have a security engineer dedicated as a resource to the project, these phases should not be labor intensive for you. The cost-ineffective way to do this is to validate systematically that design requirements are properly incorporated in the build. However, if you must review a number of projects simultaneously, the practice of validating design must be automated. You need to equip your team with the appropriate vulnerability assessment tools to verify quickly whether the build and test environments are secure. If the tool reveals a significant number of vulnerabilities, especially if you had previously specified requirements to avoid those vulnerabilities, then you take a deeper look at the system in question.

Build Phase

In the build phase:

- Ensure that various environments such as development, staging, quality assurance, and production are built with proper segmentation. Review the firewall rules if necessary.
- Ensure that proper authorizations are requested for opening up network control points (such as firewalls and routers) to meet development, administrative, and operational objectives.

- Verify that servers are built according to hardening standards.
- Ensure that your programmers exercise secure coding practices by implementing peer code reviews that check against the application security guidelines mentioned in the "Design Secure Application Architecture" section.

Test Phase

In the testing phase, the most effective way to verify the system's security posture is to conduct automated testing using security tools. Free or commercial tools are available that can be used to validate systems and applications for vulnerabilities. Note the vulnerabilities and use the project's trouble-tracking mechanism to report necessary fixes.

The Deployment Phase

The system is ready to go into production. The SDR should be focused on resolving all outstanding issues or providing a way for the project to go live with an acceptable number of exceptions. There are also activities around sanitizing development and test accounts to limit the vulnerability of rogue access. Finally, ensure that project deliverables and any confidential material are adequately secured to prevent the compromise of pertinent data.

Remediate or Grant Exceptions

The system should have passed your security vulnerability scans by this stage. If you discovered issues, they should have been escalated and remediated accordingly. If there are vulnerabilities that have not been addressed or cannot be addressed before go-live, you need to evoke the exception process to capture the risk, establish the remediation time line, and have the project sponsor sign off on the issue.

Sanitize Environments

Put the onus on the project team to identify and sanitize obsolete development, test, staging, and any other preproduction computing resource or environments. Sanitization includes changing system accounts used in development on production systems. Utilize spot-checking as a mechanism to verify quickly whether the environments are appropriately sanitized.

Secure Project Deliverables

If the project developed a custom solution that could be considered intellectual property for the company, ensure that the legal department is brought in to evaluate the organizational controls around this new solution. If other parties were involved in the development of the solution, escrow procedures around source code and intellectual property must be in place.

In addition to organizational controls, ensure that administrative and technical controls are established to secure and allow authorized revisions to the finalized source code. Also ensure that the project team secures printed and electronic project-related material. This is to prevent compromise of a system due to the extensive knowledge about the architecture found in some of these project deliverables.

The Postproduction Phase

In this phase, all the loose ends are tied up and the project goes into operations mode. The project team disbands or starts the next phase, and the operations and support teams are brought in to run the solution from a day-to-day aspect. From an SDR perspective, you need to ensure that the appropriate handoffs occur and the initial controls set forth in the requirements phase are adequately maintained over time.

Transition to Operations

Your role here is to ensure that the project has proper handoffs to maintain the controls established in the earlier phases. Review the following:

- Ensure that the user administration component has adequate controls and can be audited efficiently (see chapter 12)
- Ensure the security of *intra*organizational support. Train your support desk to give out only necessary information and authenticate callers prior to providing support.
- Ensure the security of *inter*organizational support. If the solution deployed requires support from an outside organization, define and secure the means of support (VPN, modem line, on-site access). Also, ensure that the appropriate points of contact are established and caller authentication is enforced prior to providing support.

■ Consider the implications of these new operational functions to your computer security incident response team (CSIRT). Do you need to train the administrators on CSIRT procedures? Are there interorganizational CSIRT implications involved?

An unfortunately frequent occurrence in the area of postproduction support at many organizations is that the project team does not consider the ongoing cost of support. Just a few weeks (or even days) before going live, it is not uncommon for a project team to contact the support teams to notify them that they are going live with a new system that will need to be supported. In some cases, support teams find out about their new responsibility after go-live, when something goes wrong and they are blamed for not knowing how to fix the problem.

Do not blindside your postproduction support teams. Aside from being discourteous and unfair, this can also have a significant impact on customer service and—worse yet—security. Most support teams are already fully utilized and additional work could require additional staff. Depending on the job market and the support team's budget, new head count may or may not be easy to acquire. With or without the need for additional staff, however, there will be a need for training on the new system. Contrary to popular belief, support personnel do not just "know" how to support something new; they need training.

Make sure you identify who will be involved in support and what their anticipated new work loads and tasks will be early in the project; create thorough training documentation. Then contact the managers of the support teams and let them know what is coming. Give them a chance to review the training, ask questions, schedule training for their teams, and, if needed, find new employees. In so doing, you can ensure that if a crisis happens after go-live, there will be qualified people available to address the situation, which will result in fewer frustrated customers and minimal impact to your security posture.

Change Control

Because solutions are never deployed perfectly, updates must always be made to the live system. If you have a change control board, just get a confirmation that the operations team will abide by the pre-established change process. If your company does not have a change control board, ensure that changes to be made to production systems are properly communicated, documented, and approved by the appropriate parties.

Verification of Security Posture

New solutions affect the landscape of your pre-existing security posture. Be sure to review the following:

■ Update your knowledge repository, such as the business owner, project manager, key technical lead, various touch points and dependencies, and various control points (administrative, technical, and organizational), with pertinent information from the project you just reviewed.

■ If you have an audit calendar or an annual security assessment process, be sure to include a checkpoint to review the security posture of the new project later.

■ If you have intrusion detection systems (IDS) on your network, determine whether your current coverage includes the new activities of the new solution. You may want to alert your operational team to tune the false positives that may be generated by the new system. Also, update your monitoring team on aspects of the new system that may be relevant to them.

■ If you conduct a regular vulnerability scan, you may need to update your list of servers to include the newly deployed system.

Chapter 11

Exploit Protection

What Is Exploit Protection?

"Exploit protection" is the term we use to define the function of defending your enterprise from security-related threats and vulnerabilities. A threat is a potential attack that can negatively affect the business and security posture of your enterprise. Threats capitalize on vulnerabilities in your systems, people, organizational processes, and physical security. A successful threat is defined as an exploit. An exploited organization may be affected by business disruptions, damage to its reputation, legal action, and regulatory penalties. Exploit protection is a core component of your security architecture and your second highest expenditure after personnel costs. In this chapter, we explore some cost-effective ways of addressing the challenge of building a defensive posture against security exploits.

Security Incidents and the Business

Security professionals have a tendency to implement security for security's sake. We look at the problem of viruses and we think about antivirus products. We see hackers and we think "defense in depth." In this book, we continually emphasize the need to think of security in the context of the business. How do security threats and vulnerabilities affect your company? When a hacking attempt is successful, what is the net effect of the business damage? When a self-propagating worm spreads in your network, what implications does it have for the company's core production functions? Security incidents appear on the radar screens of your executive management in essentially two forms: loss of information assets and disruption to the company's ability to do business.

Loss of Information Assets

The earlier generation of hackers was more like a group of graffiti artists. They hacked as a show of bravado and a demonstration of their technical prowess. Some of them even wore "gray hats" and alerted organizations they hacked to remediate the gaping security holes in their systems. In recent years, hacking and malicious software (malware) have morphed into an avenue for profit. Organized crime is using hackers to stockpile customer confidential information for the purpose of identity theft. Unethical businesses are using malware to SPAM or install spyware on consumer desktops. Bot or virus writers are selling their services to the highest bidder.

The brave new world of business in the digital age is fraught with a plethora of threats against information assets. Legislation is on the heels of high-publicity security incidents. More legislation means more audits and lawsuits. In the worst case, having inadequate controls to safeguard your data could lead to the demise of your business.

CardSystems could be the poster child for every company's security nightmare. Due to weak security controls, 40 million customers' credit card information was compromised. MSNBC reported that $9.24 million was spent replacing 264,000 Visa cards.[1] Aside from physical replacement costs, there were also additional costs related to customer notifications, legal fees, audits, remediation, and so on. This single incident devastated a billion-dollar company and was the main reason for its acquisition by Pay-by-Touch in December 2005.[2]

Table 11.1 outlines other high-publicity security breaches in 2005 after the Choicepoint incident. For the full list, go to www.privacyrights.org.[3]

Disruptions to the Business

Virus outbreaks have an impact on productivity and disrupt business operations that could severely cut into your company's bottom line. When the Zotob virus struck in August 2005, factory production came to a halt at a certain car company, a number of media companies scrambled to put programs on the air, administrative functions were

Table 11.1 Summary of Key Exploit Breaches by Industry in 2005

Date Made Public	Organization	Type of Breach	No. of Individuals Affected
Finance			
02.15.2005	Choicepoint	Bogus accounts established by ID thieves	145,000
02.25.2005	Bank of America	Lost backup tape	1,200,000
03.10.2005	LexisNexis	Passwords compromised	32,000
04.20.2005	Ameritrade	Lost backup tape	200,000
04.28.2005	Wachovia, Bank of America, PNC Financial, Commerce Bancorp	Dishonest insider	676,000
06.06.2005	CitiFinancial	Lost backup tape	3,900,000
06.16.2005	CardSystems	Hacking	40,000,000
12.01.2005	FirstTrust Bank	Stolen laptop	100,000
12.16.2005	La Salle Bank, ABN AMRO Mortgage Group	Backup tape with residential mortgage customer data lost in shipment by DHL	2,000,000
Retail			
03.08.2005; 04.18.2005	DSW	Hacking	1,400,000
04.14.2005	Polo Ralph Lauren	Hacking	180,000
05.02.2005	Time Warner	Lost backup tape	600,000
12.28.2005	Marriot	Lost/stolen backup tape	204,000
11.19.2005	Boeing	Stolen laptop with HR data	161,000

(*continued*)

Table 11.1 (Continued) Summary of Key Exploit Breaches by Industry in 2005

Date Made Public	Organization	Type of Breach	No. of Individuals Affected
Health care			
04.08.2005	San Jose Medical Group	Stolen computer	185,000
03.11.2005	Boston College	Hacking	120,000
Government and education			
03.11.2005	UC Berkeley	Stolen laptop	98,400
03.11.2005	Boston College	Hacking	120,000
04.01.2005	Georgia DMV	Dishonest insider	465,000
05.07.2005	Dept. of Justice	Stolen laptop	80,000
06.18.2005	University of Hawaii	Dishonest insider	150,000
07.19.2005	USC	Hacking	270,000

Source: www.privacyorg.com.

disrupted in a San Francisco Bay area airport, and ATMs stopped working at some banks. If you do not have a computer incident response process (see chapter 13), the downtime may be more significant and the damage more severe. If the virus affects customer-facing systems, your company might lose revenue, face legal action, or suffer damage to its reputation.

Zotob is just one example out of thousands of malicious software that terrorized the Internet in 2005. Sophos reports 15,907 new malware threats over the previous year—a 48 percent increase.[4] Viruses are becoming more sophisticated and they spread at ever increasing speed. Antivirus products alone cannot defend against the new blended threats.

Anatomy of Security Threats

To develop a cost-effective defense against new exploits, you need to understand the source and behavior of these threats. You need to analyze the vulnerabilities they exploit and work through a prioritization process to arrive at the most optimal defense for your organization. The cost of defending your environment will be high, so you need to have a way of balancing risk exposure against the cost to fix. Threats come from three broad sources: outsiders, insiders, and automation. The following sections describe each source in detail.

Outsider Threat

An outsider, for the purpose of this section, is defined as an individual who does not have the advantage of insider knowledge and with whom the company does not have a binding contract to hold the person liable for inappropriate use of systems. This includes cleaning crews, vendors who come in for sales or service calls, visitors to the company facilities, customers of the company, and basically anyone in the world with an Internet connection who is not employed by your company.

Potential outsider threats are defined as follows:

- Hacking from the outside is the act of penetrating the perimeter defenses of an enterprise to gain unauthorized access to systems and data, such as by using buffer overflow attacks on a public-facing Web site to gain remote access to the Web server.
- Hacking from the inside occurs when an outsider launches internal exploits by gaining physical or logical access to the internal network. The outsider could also be someone with legitimate physical access to the building, such as a vendor, customer, visitor, cleaning person, etc. An example here would be a hacker who gains wireless access into the internal network by exploiting the weakness in the wireless security infrastructure.
- A bot controller is an outsider who controls compromised machines or bots in your network by installing remote programs that activate under certain conditions. Botnets are a collection of compromised systems that can be activated by a controller to launch a coordinated attack. For example, a controller issues a command for bots to conduct a concerted distributed denial of service attack (DDoS) on a particular Web site.
- Social engineering exploits the weakness in human behavior or process to gain information or access (physical or system). A common example of a social engineering attack is when an impersonator persuades the receptionist to let him or her into the building. Social engineering attacks are typically a stepping stone to more malicious activities.
- Theft involves taking illegal possession of a physical or digital asset such as a company's backup tapes or an employee's laptop.

Hacking from the Outside

Hacking from the outside means that someone has isolated your company for a targeted attack. There could be numerous reasons why this person has your company in his or her cross hairs: your network appears to be an easy target on the hacker's automated network sweeps; your company has a high publicity site that could bring fame to the hacker; your company has information assets that could be of value to the attacker; your company's ethics contradict those of the hacker... Bottom line: Your company has been targeted.

The hacker starts with gathering pertinent data about your company using scanning tools, scouring the Internet or public directories, studying your public-facing sites or publications, conducting social engineering initiatives on your employees or partners, or going through your company's trash. When an avenue of entry is found, the hacker moves in to gain a single foothold. Once a single system is compromised (called the "zero-host"), the judicious hacker moves to download or upload tools to avoid detection. He or she then creates a secure backdoor to allow re-entry and sometimes patches the vulnerability to prevent other hackers from invading this "territory."

The next phase is to use the zero-host to compromise other systems on the internal network and search for a worthwhile "payoff." The payoff could be the theft of your confidential customer records, defacement of your Web site, disruption of your business function, or installation of malware on every vulnerable system on your network to create more bots. To find the payoff, the hacker must upload or download more tools to the zero-host and launch additional scans on the network.

Once the payoff has been identified, the hacker moves in for the kill. More attacks are launched against the target until the payoff is obtained. If you have not detected the intruder by this phase, you will have a long road of damage control ahead of you.

The following lists the common defenses against outside hacking:

- Network segmentation: Hackers get in because of holes in the perimeter security. Once inside, they find their targets because there are minimal controls to get to the business critical network segments. Hackers also exploit the lack of internal to external firewalling; this allows them to download more hacking tools to their initially compromised system or zero-host. Harden your perimeter, segment your network, and implement inside–out firewalling.
- Patch management: Hackers get in because your systems have not been patched for known vulnerabilities. Deploy a consistent,

coordinated, and predictable patch management process to update servers, desktops, laptops, and network devices with the latest system and security patches.

- System hardening: Hackers get in because your systems have out-of-the-box settings such as default passwords and unnecessary services that are vulnerable to attacks. Standardize all system builds to comply with your system-hardening guidelines. Be sure to include separate standards for hardening your bastion hosts that are directly exposed to the Internet, hardening your Web server at the presentation layer, hardening your databases, and hardening your domain controllers or authentication servers.

- Security design reviews: Hackers get in because they exploit Internet-facing Web sites or applications that have security design flaws such as not validating input, not managing sessions, not encrypting cookies, not handling errors correctly, not setting the proper levels of permission, and so on. Implementing a process for consistent review of the security designs of your business's technology initiatives provides a way to mitigate this risk.

- Intrusion detection and prevention: Hackers get in because they go undetected through the various phases of their attacks. Deploying intrusion detection at the network and host levels provides detective controls that can be triggered to alert you of a break-in. Intrusion prevention provides preventative measures to thwart the intruder and notify you in the event of an attempted hack.

- Security monitoring: Hackers get in because they can gain access without triggering the intrusion detection system (IDS) or because no one is analyzing or watching the security alerts. The challenge of wading through the considerable number of security logs (from system, network, antivirus, IDS, etc.) makes effective security monitoring a nearly impossible task. The key is to build your monitoring strategy by combining automated threat correlation with cost-effective human monitoring.

Hacking from the Inside

Hacking from the inside goes through the same phases as hacking from the outside; the difference is that the hacker has bypassed the perimeter controls (physical or logical). The advent of wireless computing has opened another vector of attack for hackers, who no longer need to gain physical access into your facilities to launch attacks against internal networks. Aside from wireless vulnerabilities, there are avenues for gaining access to wire rooms and network ports in the public receptionist areas.

Next, there are always opportunities to gain physical access to your company's facilities. Hackers can pose or even get legitimate jobs as service personnel to walk around your facilities unchallenged. The more brazen hackers may actually get employment with your company, but that would then be considered an insider attack. Regardless, the attacker is looking to bypass your perimeter security to obtain quick access to your internal network. The common defenses against internal hacking are similar to those for hacking from the outside with the following additions:

- Physical security: Hackers get in because they can gain physical access to your company's computers. Build physical security measures around access to your data systems and audit them on a regular basis. Review the surveillance tapes around the activities of your service crews on a periodic basis.
- Awareness: Hackers get in because people let them in. Educate your receptionists, end users, and security guards about social engineering.
- Wireless security: Hackers get in because they exploit weaknesses in your wireless infrastructure. Ensure that you appropriately harden, encrypt, and secure your wireless components. In addition, place a firewall behind your wireless access point and only allow known end points.
- Network admissions control (NAC): Hackers get in because they may be able to gain physical access and plug into active ports on the network. Ensure that ports, especially in nonsecured areas, only allow access to valid devices and credentials. An NAC solution prevents anyone from plugging a laptop into an open port and gaining undeterred and undetected access to the internal network. Additionally, the NAC can be used to enforce end-point security levels by quarantining noncompliant end points until all relevant security and system patches are installed before letting them into the network.

Bot Controllers

Another mechanism that outsiders use to gain access from the inside is to become bot controllers. A bot controller is someone who has remote control over a number of systems in your network. Bot-focused hackers who compromise a system will install a zombie program designed to be difficult to detect that can be activated under certain conditions to execute the malicious intent of the bot controller. A compromised machine that can be controlled externally is called a bot. To be a bot controller, the hacker must have successfully hacked through your perimeter defense and found a range of vulnerable systems to compromise. Also typical with bot-related attacks is the use of other file transfer, scanning, propagation, and backdoor tools. These attacks combine to form what is called a blended threat. The intent of the intruder is to automate the propagation of bots in a compromised environment. The following defenses are available for bot-related attacks:

- Host security: Zombies get installed because they are not detected or blocked at the host level. Updated antivirus software on your host should detect and quarantine malware from being installed on your machines. Host firewalls should block bots from getting in or going out. Host-based IDS or intrusion prevention systems (IPS) should detect and prevent bot-related attacks.
- Intrusion detection and prevention: Hackers get in because they are undetected. Bots, especially those that run a blended threat rootkit (packaged hacker tools), generate significant amounts of network traffic. IDS and IPS should detect and prevent the initial hack and any subsequent bot communication back to the controller.
- Inside–out firewalling: Bots communicate back to their controller because they are not blocked. Inside–out firewalling (discussed later in this chapter) prevents nonstandard traffic from going back out as well as blocks the uploading and downloading of files from the inside to the Internet.
- Network segmentation: Bots automatically infect other machines because they can scan, compromise, and upload files to them. Segmenting your network prevents and limits the activities of bot-related attacks.
- Vulnerability scanning: Bots can lie dormant because they are undetected. They typically have a response mechanism to receive orders from the bot controller. A regular vulnerability scan of your network should test for the presence of bots before they are activated by the controller.
- Patch management: Systems get compromised because they are not patched. Patched systems are more resilient to interactive and automated attacks.

Social Engineering

Social engineering is basically conman artistry in the context of information security. Today, there is also another form of social engineering called *phishing* that lures victims to click on malicious links through e-mail or instant messaging that would lead to some form of compromise (typically, the theft of credentials or credit card information). Social engineering is not a one-time activity for a hacker trying to get to a big payoff. If the hacker cannot penetrate your perimeter security, he or she may use social engineering to gain legitimate physical access to your internal network by getting your receptionist to let him or her into the facility. During the payoff search phase, the hacker may social engineer the IT help desk to reset a certain password to the target computer. Social engineering exploits the weakness in human behavior; the only countermeasure to this is a pragmatic and effective security awareness and training program, as described in chapter 6.

Theft

Theft is the oldest form of attack. From an information security perspective, you are concerned about the loss of information assets. If an unencrypted backup tape is stolen, you may be entangled in a long process of notification, litigation, and remediation activities. If a network administrator's laptop containing your entire security architecture and other core critical IT data is stolen, you may need to bolster your compensating controls to account for proprietary data that could now be public. A sound encryption strategy, a strong awareness program, and good physical security measures are your pillars of defense against stolen or lost information assets.

Insider Threats

It is often noted that the majority of security incidents stem from the inside. According to the 2005 CSI/FBI Annual Computer Crime and Security Survey, the percentage is closer to 50/50.[5] However, what is not reflected in these numbers is the increased potential damage of an insider attack. The insider has authorized physical and systems access, knows about the business, can easily identify the most lucrative target, has relationships with other employees, and potentially knows the extent of your security measures. The insider attack is one of the most challenging threats to defend against.

It is also important to note that there are two types of insider threats: malicious and unintentional. The malicious insider has a motive, typically financial gain or revenge, and attacks the company's ability to do business or steals information assets in a premeditated and calculated fashion. The unintentional insider has no motive but jeopardizes the company's information or systems out of convenience, user error, negligence, or ignorance. The different types of insider threats are defined as follows:

- Hacking from inside involves an insider with authorized physical and network access who launches internal exploits against internal systems. The insider could be an employee, consultant, contractor, business partner, or outsourcer. Hacking techniques include scanning, snooping, installation of backdoors, and so on. For example, a contractor with limited access launches vulnerability assessment tools to discover weaknesses in the company's customer databases.
- Theft involves taking illegal possession of a physical or digital asset. For example, a database administrator uses a service account to download customer information onto a thumb drive.
- Social engineering exploits the weakness in human behavior or process to gain information or access (physical or system). Typically, this is a stepping stone to more malicious activities. For example, an insider manipulates a database administrator to give him or her the service account logon to the company's core critical databases.
- In collaborative attacks, an insider works with outsiders or other insiders to siphon off critical information assets or disrupt the company's business. For example, an insider working with an identity theft ring installs a program that regularly transfers confidential customer data to an FTP site on the Internet.
- Former employee attacks comprise current outsiders with insider knowledge who have malicious intent toward the company. For example, a recently terminated employee who still has legitimate remote access because it was not deactivated logs in and plants a self-propagating worm in the company's network.
- Lost information assets involve an employee, consultant, contractor, business partner, or outsourcer who loses an asset that contains confidential or proprietary data. For example, a contractor working on the HR system loses a laptop that has the company's employee roster.

- User error and ignorance is an unintentional mistake or action that causes downtime to the business or loss of confidential data. For example, a programming error exposes an entire database table of customer data on a Web site as opposed to only selected fields.
- In irresponsible use, a user breaks protocol for convenience or personal interest, jeopardizing the company's data in the process. For example, a user allows his or her friends to use the company laptop for online poker, which typically involves the installation of software that could be potentially malicious.

Hacking from the Inside

Hacking from inside is a significant threat that can often go undetected for extended periods of time. This is largely due to the amount of knowledge the insider has about the systems, network, and the people who manage them. Insiders can also bring in tools downloaded from home and upload them to their company computer via the CD or DVD-ROM drive or through a USB-based thumb drive, and run any hacking utilities against internal systems. In many cases, they may have physical access to workstations or even data centers to mount direct attacks on your infrastructure. Here are some recommended defenses against insiders:

- Background checks and behavioral interviews: Insiders get employed because of lackadaisical employment practices. Conduct thorough background checks and include behavioral tests or questions in interviews.
- Awareness and governance: Insiders succeed because they are not discouraged, deterred, or monitored. Awareness plays an important role in cultivating a security-conscious culture. The human factor is typically labeled as the weakest link in security. However, an effective awareness and governance program could condition human behavior to serve your organization's security posture. If managers are given the proper training to pay attention to tell-tale signs of a potential insider hacker, they could take preemptive strikes to prevent a significant breach. If the general user population frowns upon a casual attitude toward security, an insider would hesitate to act for fear of being caught. If those who engage in improper behavior— whether malicious or unintentional—are held accountable for

their actions, then others would take note not to behave in the same way.

- NAC: Insiders can bring in their own hacking laptops to connect to the network. NAC prevents any unauthorized end point from connecting and provides an audit log of authorized connections.
- Identity and access management (I&AM): Insiders can get access to data or systems that have nothing to do with their job functions due to the mismanagement of access. I&AM, which is further discussed in chapter 12, minimizes the risk of unnecessary access by enforcing the "least privilege" principle—the idea that a person should have only the necessary privileges to perform his or her job functions and nothing more.
- Security review and audit: Insiders can operate indefinitely because they can go undetected due to the lack of reviews. Conduct periodic reviews of access to critical data and systems.
- Physical security: Insiders can get physical access to exploit servers that are not protected by adequate physical access control. Ensure that all critical servers are locked in a room or a cabinet and that access to that location is auditable. Conduct regular audits of data center access and lock out wiring rooms such as the intermediate distribution frames (IDFs) and main distribution frames (MDFs). Review the surveillance tapes around the activities of your personnel to detect suspicious behavior.
- Intrusion detection and prevention: Insiders succeed because their hacking activities are undetected. Insiders who cannot get proper credentials to their target system through nontechnical means, such as social engineering, can use hacking tools to facilitate their attacks. IDS and IPS devices that are strategically placed in the internal network can detect and prevent known (if the IDS/IPS is signature based) or new (if the IDS/IPS is anomaly based) hacking activities.
- Network segmentation: Insiders succeed because they can gain remote access to their target systems. A sound network segmentation strategy should at least have the following separations: DMZ, back-end production, nonproduction, end-user computing, and administrative. The proper separation of networks creates barriers for the insider hacker to reach his or her target destination. To overcome these barriers, the hacker would need to perform more malicious activities, which increases his or her visibility as well as the chances of getting caught.

Theft

Theft from an insider is probably the attack vector that you will encounter the most. Insiders have authorized access to valuable information assets as part of their job functions. Credit card processors see credit card numbers all day long. Loan processors and officers have full access to their customers' financial histories and Social Security numbers. Database or data warehouse administrators have "the keys to the kingdom" as far as information assets go. Because they have legitimate access, there is no need for hacking. The following defenses are available for data theft:

- Host security: Insiders can steal data because they can easily export data out of your systems. Deploy host security features that prevent users from off-loading data, such as locking out the use of the floppy drive, USB ports, CD/DVD drive, etc. Provide solutions for users to share files via the network and allow the use of USB flash drives judiciously.
- Physical security: Insiders can steal digital or physical assets if they are accessible and there is little or no deterrence. Promoting the locking up and shredding of confidential data and reviewing surveillance periodically would curb these unwanted activities.
- Security review and audit: Insiders who have authorized access can steal information assets indefinitely due to the lack of review. Conduct periodic reviews of access to critical data and systems.
- Segregation of duties: Even users with privileged access who legitimately need it might not need as much as they have. Look for ways to segregate administrators so that no single individual has access to all the servers or databases. Also, be sure to assign unique IDs to all administrators or implement mechanisms such as "switch user" (su) in UNIX to ensure accountability of privileged access use. If everyone shares the administrator or DBA account, there can be no consequences for misuse because it will not be traceable.
- Job rotation: Rotate your employees across their job functions so that if someone is doing something malicious, he or she will cease to have the ability for an extended period of time. Job rotation has the added benefit of keeping your employees from getting bored and ensuring that more people are cross-trained. This enables your operations to continue if someone suddenly leaves the company or falls ill for an extended period of time.

Social Engineering

Social engineering for insiders is comparable to that for outsiders with the added advantage of getting more pertinent data or access. Insiders know the right people to chat up or manipulate and they know their target. Similar to the defense for outsider social engineering, an effective security awareness program keeps your employees on the alert for social engineering traits.

Collaborative Attacks

Collaborative attacks add a layer of complexity to the insider problem. The insider is basically colluding with other insiders or outsiders to operate a malicious initiative. The majority of these collusions is financially motivated and involves theft of information assets. There is a chance that some attackers are out to take down business functions as well. Protection against collusion is similar to the preventative and detective controls listed under hacking from the inside, theft, and social engineering. The bottom line is to prevent the insider from being effective. There is no defense for preventing insiders from interacting with other insiders or outsiders.

Former Employees

Former employees have information about the company that could be used to launch a more targeted attack. The ex-employee could have even planted a backdoor prior to his or her departure. The defenses against this type of attack are encapsulated in the recommendations for outsider threats with the addition of I&AM. Due to ineffective I&AM, ex-employees can get remote or physical access to data or systems even after they have been terminated. I&AM, discussed in chapter 12, must pay special attention to terminations, especially if the employee has access to sensitive systems or data.

Lost Information Assets, User Error and Ignorance, Irresponsible Use

Information assets can be lost or stolen. This is largely due to insider negligence as opposed to malicious intent. Users can also be irresponsible or ignorant about the seriousness of information assets under their care. The protection that can be offered to minimize the implications of user irresponsibility or ignorance is as follows:

■ Host security: A person who recovers or steals a physical asset can obtain valuable data due to the lack of security around the lost property. Irresponsible insiders can allow their friends to use their work laptops because there are no consequences to their actions. All mobile devices such as laptops, personal digital assistants (PDAs), cell phones, etc. that contain sensitive company data should be password protected, hardened, and encrypted. Mobile devices should be locked down to allow only business use. This includes not giving users permission to install unnecessary or unlicensed software. Additionally, a tracking device should be installed on mobile devices to enable the recovery of lost or stolen property or an autodestruct feature should be enabled on PDAs so that if the device is lost or stolen, a signal can be sent to destroy all data on the device permanently.

■ Awareness and accountability: Users lose their belongings or act irresponsibly because they are not made aware of or held liable for the damage caused by their negligence. Create awareness initiatives that educate the users on the importance of protecting information assets. Develop and enforce policies that hold users accountable for the loss or mishandling of information assets.

Automated Attacks

This book makes a distinction between automated hacker tools and automated attacks. Automated hacker tools are categorized as part of the arsenal of tools that a hacker uses to break into a system. These tools include automated scanning engines, automated rootkits, brute force attack functionality, and so on.

In contrast, automated threats are described as fire-and-forget types of malicious threats. Automated attacks are the weapons of choice for malicious individuals who want to affect a significant number of systems in a short period of time. These threats are described as follows:

■ A virus is a program that has malicious intent and is designed to mass propagate. For example, the Bagle virus opens a backdoor, lowers the security settings of computers it infects, and propagates itself via mass e-mails.

- SPAM or SPIM is an automated unsolicited mass e-mail (SPAM) or instant message (SPIM) that can be autogenerated by the millions. SPAM is frequently used by Internet mass marketers to promote their products.
- Spyware is a covert program that records user activity, scours for useful data, or subverts normal computer operations without the user's consent. A common application of spyware is to install a keylogger and send the resulting keystroke data to a specified e-mail address.
- Denial of service (DOS) cripples a system's ability to function by overloading it—for example, using botnets to SPAM a company's mail server, thereby crippling its e-mail capability.

Viruses

Viruses continue to wreak havoc on businesses year after year. The advent of blended threats and the speed in which they spread have created significant challenges within the security community. The viruses of today typically have four phases: exploit, infect, propagate, and activate. Exploit is the first phase where the virus capitalizes on certain vulnerabilities in a system in an attempt to infect the system. Next, the virus compromises the system and starts up its propagation mechanism. The propagation mechanism consists of a way to select additional targets, scan for them, and infect them by exploiting the same vulnerabilities. Simultaneously, the virus also activates its "payload" or acts on the malicious intent of the virus writer. The payload could be a distributed denial of service attack on a certain site, the displaying of a banner message to all users, or the destruction of data on the system. The pillars of defense against virus or worm outbreaks are:

- Patch management: Viruses spread due to the vast numbers of vulnerable hosts available for infection. Viruses usually come out days or weeks after a certain vulnerability or patch is announced. Patching of hosts and servers prevents the infection of viruses that exploit these published weaknesses.
- Antivirus solution: Viruses get in and spread because they are not blocked or quarantined at the gateways or at the hosts. An effective antivirus architecture protects the perimeter, the e-mail gateways, the servers, the workstations, and the laptops. Ensure that your antivirus solution updates on a daily basis. This stops the virus from propagating and infecting other machines.

- NAC: Viruses get in through uncontrolled access to internal networks. A vendor, consultant, or mobile employee could contract a virus from outside and infect the internal network just by plugging into a port at the office the next day. An effective NAC architecture protects against unknown devices plugging into the network (such as laptops from vendors, contractors, or other outsiders) and only allows approved devices with the appropriate security controls to connect to the network (quarantines and redirects unpatched devices to download appropriate patches).

- Network segmentation: Viruses from end-user segments can cripple production systems due to the lack of segmentation. Creating partitions in your network allows you to contain the spread of the viruses to core critical systems and infrastructure.

- Disabling local administrator rights: Viruses can infect machines because many users run with administrative privileges. During the infect and propagation phases, viruses typically have to overwrite files, install programs, or instantiate pre-existing commands on the system. Removing local administrator rights prevents the virus from accessing key folders, files, and executables on your systems, thus breaking its infection and propagation capabilities.

- Host security: Viruses spread because they can infect other hosts. Host security features such as firewalls, antivirus, and host-based IDS or IPS can contain viruses at the host level and prevent them from spreading to other hosts. Hosts that have firewall protection can also block out infection attempts against them.

- Intrusion detection, threat correlation engine, and incident response: Viruses spread because they have time to propagate. An IDS that is monitored regularly or a threat correlation engine that interprets anomalous activities on the network can allow for early detection of a virus infection. Some correlation engines can even pinpoint the source of the virus and the targets that have been infected. Detection allows you to activate your incident response team to isolate and contain the virus quickly.

- Security lab: Viruses continue to spread because responders to the event do not understand how the virus works. Building a security lab that provides a "sandbox" environment in which security professionals can watch the various phases of the virus will provide your incident response team with solutions to contain and eradicate the virus. Some companies rely heavily on their antivirus vendors to provide solutions. This could lead to the continual spread of the virus due to possible vendor delays in finding a resolution that works for all their customers. Additionally, some viruses are designed to morph to be resilient against signature-based antivirus defenses. The lab allows you to understand your specific strain of virus and discover a remediation without waiting for your antivirus vendor.

■ Backup and restore: The impact of a virus is prolonged due to the inability of the business to recover lost data or configurations. Backup and restore are key defenses against a virus because viruses have payloads that maliciously disrupt the system's ability to function. Backup and restore are important events in your recovery phase for two main reasons. First, you need to restore your system configurations and data to a state prior to the virus attack. Second, you can overwrite an infected system with a clean copy to eliminate the presence of the virus from your environment. It is critical to have a strong backup and restore strategy and to test frequently. Most companies find out too late that their backup processes fail regularly, and when they look to restore data, they find nothing from which to do so.

SPAM and SPIM

SPAM and SPIM are essentially used to attack productivity. SPAM floods your e-mail systems and causes your end users to sift through unnecessary mail to get to their work mail or it causes them to linger on the SPAM content, which is also a productivity issue. SPAM has been extended to the instant messaging environment in the form of SPIM—same attack, different medium. Recently, SPAM has been combined with phishing attacks to lure users to Web sites that could compromise data or your systems. Defenses against SPAM and SPIM include:

■ Anti-SPAM filters: SPAM gets in because there is nothing to block it at the e-mail gateway or client. Deploy an anti-SPAM architecture that automatically updates new keywords and techniques to filter out SPAM.

■ Approved instant messaging: SPIM gets in because users have uncontrolled instant messaging at the workplace. If instant messaging is approved in your company, deploy an enterprise-grade instant messaging system that has encryption, auditing, and filtering to protect against SPIM, virus attacks, and loss of information assets.

■ Awareness: SPAM is in part the result of end users giving out their work e-mail address. Raise the awareness that users should not give out their work e-mail address to conduct personal affairs. Once an e-mail address ends up on one SPAM list, it will exponentially pass on to other lists, causing the user to receive SPAM at work. Users should also be taught to ignore SPAM. Many users try to remove themselves from SPAM mailing lists by clicking on the link in the e-mail that claims to be the unsubscribe feature. What most users do not know is that, unlike with legitimate e-mails where the unsubscribe feature actually works, with SPAM e-mails, clicking the unsubscribe link does the opposite. Rather than removing the user from the mailing list, it confirms the user's e-mail as valid and flags it for additional distribution and mailings.

Spyware

Spyware is an attack on productivity and could potentially result in the compromise of confidential data. Distinctions are made between spyware and adware. Spyware installs covert applications on the victim's system; adware simply overwhelms the victim with ad banners. Regardless, you want to prevent these issues in your environment, so here are some recommendations:

■ Host security: Spyware infects your systems because it obtains installation rights from the users who are running in administrator mode. By hardening your hosts and restricting the use of local administrator rights, you can prevent the propagation of spyware.
■ Antivirus solution: Spyware infects your system because it is not detected or quarantined. Most enterprise-grade antivirus solutions include spyware protection. Check with your vendor on getting an update that detects, quarantines, and removes spyware.
■ Web filtering: Spyware infects your systems because your end users can browse to inappropriate sites. Legitimate business Web sites do not propagate spyware. Use a Web-filtering gateway to prevent your users from going to nonbusiness Web sites that prompt or manipulate users into installing spyware.
■ Awareness: Spyware infects your systems because users are duped into installing the malicious code. You may not be able to block every malicious Web site with a Web-filtering engine. Educate your user community on productivity, the risks of installing unknown software, and the dangers of visiting dubious Web sites.

Denial of Service

DOS attacks have been around for several years. Although this is still a viable attack, most companies have largely defended against them by procuring new DOS-resistant network devices, building redundancy into their networks, and monitoring their bandwidth for DOS attacks.

Cost Management and Exploit Protection

Looking at the cost of the long list of available defense mechanisms and comparing it against your limited budget, you need to decide where best to spend your exploit protection dollars. Refer to chapter 9 for a way to prioritize your risk mitigation initiatives. In the following sections, we address some common defensive components and elaborate on how to deploy them cost effectively.

Inside–Out Firewalling

The deployment of perimeter firewalls is the most fundamental element of any business network. Most organizations have outside to inside (outside–in) firewalling that prevents all but a limited range of legitimate traffic into the "demilitarized zone" (DMZ) or internal networks. The obvious benefit of this is that outside–in firewalling protects the company from attacks that originate from the outside. Ports that are typically opened are HTTP and secure socket layer (SSL) for Web traffic, domain name service (DNS) ports for resolution of IP addresses, e-mail ports, remote access connections, and a handful of other necessary business-to-business communication (file transfer or virtual private network) protocols.

However, the adoption of inside to outside (inside–out) firewalling is not as prevalent. Many companies have limited or no inside–out firewall rules, thus allowing broad access for outbound connections from within their corporate network to the outside world. A cost-efficient way to hinder the effectiveness of malware significantly is to focus on implementing inside–out firewalling. You already own the firewalls, so stretch your investment dollars by configuring them to enable the following:

- Block viruses from spreading from one segment of your network to another or from your network to other companies, thus limiting your liability and containing the exponential propagation of the virus.
- Limit the ability for automated attacks to download more tools from the Internet.

- Prevent spyware, zombies, or bots from establishing contact or sending data to their controllers (person or group who collects or controls the malware).
- Enforce stronger end-user policies to limit business-only access from inside your network to the Internet. This in turn should lower your infection rate as well as curb undesirable, unproductive, and potentially malicious behavior.

To facilitate inside–out firewalling, activate firewall monitoring to see the range of traffic going to the Internet from your network. You will be surprised to find the amount of nonbusiness-related and potentially malware-associated activities traversing your perimeter. From the firewall logs, establish and enforce your policies around a limited range of business- and IT-sanctioned activities such as Internet browsing, DNS resolution, network time protocol (NTP), and so on.

Inside–out firewalling is not a silver bullet, but rather another layer of defense that you can leverage without additional hardware. Sophisticated malware writers still get around these controls by tunneling their traffic through legitimate inside–out ports such as HTTP or even SSL. Talk to your firewall vendors about how your specific firewall can counter the inside–out threats that use legitimate ports.

Intrusion Detection and Prevention

Host-based as well as network-based intrusion detection systems suffer from the following disadvantages:

- IDSs typically yield a high amount of false positives triggered by legitimate traffic on your network and systems. Resources must be dedicated to research and tune your IDS on a regular basis to make it functional. Parsing through the noise generated by these innocuous alerts to identify real security events proves to be a continual challenge for most organizations.
- Active monitoring of IDS is a significant drain on resources. The promise of IDS is early detection of malicious activities. To do that, you have the option of staffing resources 24/7/365 (or outsourcing the function) to monitor network IDS, or to set up an automated alerting (paging) mechanism. Otherwise, you fall back on reactive monitoring, which is to have one resource analyze IDS logs from the day before to spot suspicious events.

■ The cost factor to host-based IDS is high due to the per-seat pricing model typical in this arena. For every server, workstation, and laptop you want to protect, there is a host IDS cost associated with it.

Let us also evaluate the issues around intrusion prevention systems.

■ IPS is intrusive by nature and may disrupt business. Unless you have a stable network with minimal changes, deploying IPS could work against your resiliency and be the cause of business downtime.

■ IPS is high maintenance. You must constantly tune your IPS to adapt to the dynamic nature of your network and systems. You also must dedicate resources to identify and fix potential IPS-related issues. Basically, IPS will be in the line of fire every time there is an unaccountable outage on the network or system. If you deploy host-based IPS (H-IPS), you need to include it in the testing life cycle of every project due to the potential nuances it may have on identifying legitimate system calls as incidents. You must dedicate resources to troubleshoot with developers or system engineers to weed out H-IPS as the cause of issues.

From a cost-versus-risk perspective, you need to ask the question of whether the protection offered by IDS and IPS is worth the price of deployment and ongoing maintenance. Here are some guidelines around pragmatic approaches to IDS and IPS:

■ Deal with the high count of false positives by looking into a correlation engine. There are different flavors of this technology from all the major vendors, but basically the idea is built around a central repository that takes in logs or events from various security devices (firewalls, IDS, system logs) and applies a layer of heuristics to the data to determine the validity of a security event. Some correlation engines will go as far as to incorporate a network scanning application to actively verify that the vulnerability actually exists. This is a worthwhile investment considering the significant cost savings that can be gleaned from the resource hours needed to do similar types of correlation manually, consistently, and constantly.

■ Calculate the cost of switching to a managed service provider (MSP) if you are currently operating your IDS in-house. Intrusion detection is one of the most viable candidates for MSP due to the sheer resource commitment needed to monitor events 24/7/365 and some clear advantages that you cannot obtain internally.

- One key benefit of using an MSP for intrusion detection is that it monitors threats across the nation (maybe the world) and you may be able to benefit from early notification of developing issues before they hit your area.

- Second, it has dedicated staff who specialize in monitoring and can more accurately weed out false positives and identify real events. You can make use of the staff as an extension of your security organization by leveraging their subject matter expertise.

- Third, some MSPs offer guarantees to provide you with timely notification and acceptable service levels, and they will often share some of the risk with your company if an incident does occur.

- Fourth, you have more flexibility in tailoring your intrusion-detection offerings if you need to scale appropriately or when you are not getting satisfactory results from your provider. MSPs are accommodating and are typically willing to work with you to put together a package that meets your needs. If you have IDS deployed, some of them are willing to monitor and manage your pre-existing IDS. If you do not have IDS, they can lease or include physical devices as part of your monthly fees.

- A key thing to consider when selecting an intrusion-detection MSP is to ask for dedicated resources. Make sure that you have the same group of people watching your network rather than a rotating staff. Also, ask to have direct access to that dedicated group as opposed to going through several levels of support before talking to a skilled person. Choose an MSP that provides written guarantees and appealing service level agreements (SLAs).

- Finally, negotiate an "out" clause in your contract so that when the MSP fails to meet expectations continually, you can select another provider without getting locked in for the entire term of the contract (MSPs usually want at least two or three years).

If you do not have resources to procure a correlation engine or engage and intrusion-detection MSP, look into leveraging other parts of your company for 24/7/365 monitoring. Work through executive management to inculcate security roles into the jobs of network operations center (NOC) teams, system administrators, database administrators, and any personnel who have their eyes on the real-time status of your network, systems, or applications.

IPS is a case-by-case type of technology. If you have a stable network with minimal changes or a strict change control process, it may be a viable solution for you. If you have tuned your correlation engine to a point where the false-positive count is virtually zero, then by all means deploy IPS. We recommend selective deployment of IPS in strategic areas that are not in the core network route to avoid the potential of major disruptions. As a side note, there are some intrusion-protection MSPs that provide guarantees around 100 percent accuracy of their IPS devices, but we would advise you to read the abundant fine print attached to that claim.

Patch Management—System Resiliency

"Sophos research shows that connecting an unprotected, unpatched computer running Windows XP (without SP2) to the Internet leads to a 40% risk of infection from an Internet worm within about 10 minutes, rising to a 94% chance after 60 minutes."[6] Self-propagating worms and viruses typically appear days after the public announcement of vulnerabilities. The risk of not patching your systems in short order could have serious implications due to the speed and fury of virus outbreaks in recent months. For example, in 2005, Zotob took five days to hit after the patch was released; in 2000, Nimda struck systems a year after the vulnerability was announced. Table 11.2 shows how dramatically the elapsed time from virus creation to virus outbreak has decreased in five years.

Table 11.2 Exploit Time Frames

Virus/Worm	Microsoft Critical Patch	Date Patch Issued	Exploit Date	Time Frame to Patch
Nimda	MS 00-078	10.17.2000	9.18.2001	336 days
Slammer	MS 02-039	7.24.2002	1.25.2003	183 days
Blaster	MS 03-026	7.16.2003	8.11.2003	26 days
Sasser	MS 04-011	4.13.2004	5.1.2004	18 days
Zotob	MS 05-039	8.9.2005	8.13.2005	5 days

This table lists five of the top worms that hit between the 2001 and 2005, the Microsoft critical patch number, the date Microsoft issued each patch, the date the worm was actually exploited, and the amount of time that companies had to patch their systems to ensure they were protected (time frame to patch = exploit date − date patch issued). Notice the precipitous decline in the time frame to patch.

Patch management is not an easy path to navigate in any company. The common complaints about patching include:

■ Patches cause instability in systems and must be sufficiently tested prior to their release into production. Administrators or security personnel often get the blame for any system woes after a patch is deployed.

■ Most patches require system reboot, which adds to the instability factor and causes downtime to business functions. Closely tied to this is the issue of identifying a maintenance window for patching.

■ Patching affects every system. Due to its wide ranging impact at the server, workstation, and laptop levels, patching requires significant coordination and buy-in from a large number of stakeholders. Not only do administrators need to take into consideration the variants of operating systems, database systems, and network devices, but in many cases they also need to consider the applications or processes running on each component.

■ There are too many patches, many of which are irrelevant to any given environment. *SC Magazine* reported a total of 3,780 patches in the first two quarters of 2005.[7]

To counter the stigma associated with patching, focus on building an effective patch management process (PMP) with these practical guidelines:

■ Publicize the objectives of your PMP to executives and management. The key message to carry across is that patching is a necessity that every company faces. Because there are no options not to patch, the goal of the PMP is to make patching a predictable, reliable, and efficient process. Predictability is realized by adhering to a set patching schedule. Reliability is achieved by having the proper testing processes as well as the right staff on hand after the patch has been deployed to validate the system processes and to support any potential issues that may arise. Efficiency is gained by tuning the PMP with each iterative cycle to make it more seamless and less disruptive to the business. When faced with resistance, emphasize that a planned downtime with reliable personnel on staff to bring the systems back up (as well as contingency plans) is more desirable than an unplanned downtime and potential loss of systems or data caused by a security breach.

■ Establish the roles and responsibilities of all the parties involved in the PMP. Your patching should cover servers, workstations, and laptops and include network devices as well. Gather key representatives from each group to form a patch management committee (PMC) that makes joint decisions on patching strategies and contributes to the continual improvement of the PMP.

■ Create contingency plans for patching. Work with the PMC to formulate rollback and communications plans in the event that the patch proves problematic. What we have found in most organizations is that patches are often the culprit of a system failure. A patch, however, may root out a deficiency in the way an application communicates with the kernel causing it to choke. Set the right expectations with the appropriate parties to work on improving problematic systems rather than reverse the patch application.

■ Establish a regular maintenance window for patching following the week of Microsoft's Patch Tuesday (regular patching cycle). As noted in table 11.2, virus writers are moving at unprecedented speed to produce malware as soon as five days after the patch is released; the term "zero-day" exploit has ceased to be as theoretical as it once was. Allocate testing for the four days following Patch Tuesday and set the target of patching production over that weekend.

■ Involve your change management committee or board. Patching requires the appropriate approvals because it has a wide-ranging impact to all systems in the enterprise. Ensure that you embed the PMP into the monthly routine of the change control meetings.

■ Create an exception procedure. There will be business or IT managers whose initiatives will result in your inability to patch their systems. Put the onus on them to inform the PMC at the change control meetings. Review and grant these exceptions accordingly. Set a cutoff date for the list of systems to be exempt and set expectations of the requestor as to when the systems on the exception list will be patched.

- Include an emergency PMP (EPMP). There will be critical patches that must be applied sooner rather than later due to impending attacks. In those cases, evoke the EPMP and rush the patching through in no more than two days.

A successful PMP saves you from significant hours of downtime and damage control.

Local Administrator Rights

A zero-day virus is malware that infects computers before a protection (i.e., signature-based antivirus update) against it is known. Preventing your normal end users from being local administrators on their work computers is probably your least expensive defense against zero-day viruses. Most malware relies on the user's administrative privilege to write or install malicious programs to the system folder or registry. By giving the user a nonprivileged account, a variety of malware would fail to infect the host computer.

Removing local administrative rights has other security benefits, such as preventing users from installing nonapproved software or devices. Users would need to get the appropriate approvals to have company-licensed software pushed out to them. However, this may also be a source of contention due to the limitation of printer or other types of installations that require administrative rights. Users who are used to getting their way are not going to welcome this change in policy. Be sure to get the proper executive support, especially from the business side, to push such an initiative. Provide alternatives to approved installations by creating scripts that allow users to run as administrators while they are logged in as a nonprivileged account.

Other solutions allow you to right-click and send installation files to an administrator stand-in application to facilitate the installation. This method allows you to present a warning banner to inform the users of their responsibilities. Both administrator substitute options require you to provide end users with an administrative password. To ensure the proper safeguarding of this privilege, change the password on a regular basis and communicate that to your end-user support teams.

Exploit Protection and Security Operations

In this chapter, we looked at the business reasons for managing threats and vulnerabilities. We analyzed the different vectors of attack and recommended defensive and preventative controls to mitigate these potential threats. Viruses are growing more sophisticated and the rise of identity theft by organized crime will continue to make exploit protection a challenging endeavor in your enterprise. You cannot secure everything, but you need to have a process to cover your risks systematically over time as well as have a defense when a security incident happens.

The basic strategy is to conduct an annual risk assessment (as outlined in chapter 9) and identify high-priority risk areas prior to planning for your next year's budget. Use the results of your risk assessment to put the onus of prioritizing risks on your executive management team. Once you have your controls in place, you need a strategy to keep them at acceptable levels. Controls typically deteriorate over time if they are not properly monitored or updated. Maintaining these controls is a topic that we will explore in section 5.

References

1. http://www.msnbc.msn.com/id/9443546/from/RL.1/
2. http://biz.yahoo.com/prnews/051209/sff033.html?. v=24
3. http://www.privacyrights.org/ar/ChronDataBreaches.htm
4. http://www.sophos.com/pressoffice/news/articles/ 2005/12/toptensummary05.html
5. http://www.cybercrime.gov/FBI2005.pdf
6. http://www.sophos.com/pressoffice/news/articles/ 2005/12/toptensummary05.html
7. http://www.scmagazine.com/uk/news/article/523151/developing- patch-vulnerability-management-strategy/

Section 5

SECURITY OPERATIONS— MAINTAINING SECURITY EFFICIENTLY

Security operations is the area with the largest ongoing expense in the security department. That is why it is crucial to ensure that your operations are efficient. Having efficient operations actually meets two goals:

- Ensuring that you are getting the most out of your security operations budget
- Making it easy for operations personnel to do their jobs accurately, thereby ensuring that you can maintain your enhanced security posture over time

To this point, this book has been laying the foundation for your security operations. First, you learned how to develop a strategy, and then you learned how to implement it procedurally and technically. You also learned that the output of many of your security projects included some ongoing tasks that must be executed manually or automatically for the life of a particular system or, indeed, the life of your organization.

This section focuses on two key areas of security operations that are fed by the myriad security projects driven by your strategy: identity and access management (chapter 12) and incident response (chapter 13). These operational areas are important not only because they are so broad and complex, but also because together they comprise the basis for your key controls. As a result, security operations are the most scrutinized area of a company when it is audited.

Identity and access management were discussed architecturally in chapter 10, "Security Design Review." In chapter 12, "Identity and Access Management," we present an approach to maximizing the efficiency of your user management processes irrespective of their current state of automation. We also provide guidance on how to document and report your user management activities as part of making the audit function operational.

In chapters 9 and 11, we discussed how to identify, remediate, and prevent key vulnerabilities. But remediation and prevention initiatives can take a while to implement, and new exploits are discovered each day. The media is full of talk these days about "zero day" exploits, in which a new threat spreads globally on the day that it is invented. In this scenario, there is no time for anyone to react with antivirus updates, patches, or any other solution. Thus, there will always be a chance that you will get hit with something. Hopefully, you have designed your security architecture in such a way that the damage is limited, but damage could still occur. In chapter 13, "Cost-Effective Incident Response," we discuss the operational component of handling risks: what to do when a vulnerability is exploited. A well-defined incident response process saves your company significant amounts of downtime and damage control expenditures.

Chapter 12

Identity and Access Management

Introduction

"Identity and access management" (I&AM) is the phrase most commonly used in the information security industry to describe processes and technologies that allow an organization to identify accurately who their users are and what resources they are able to access. In a small company, managing users can be almost trivial, although even small companies struggle if they have a lot of resources. In a large company or any company that makes heavy use of temporary workers or contractors, managing users can be a daily nightmare.

From an audit perspective, effectively managing users is the key to comfort. After all, if users cannot access resources that do not pertain to them, the likelihood that those resources contain legitimate data increases dramatically. Also, having appropriate access controls implies that there is adequate segregation of duties, which gives the auditors comfort that fraud is effectively avoided.

Describing identity and access management is simple, and anyone can paint a very neat picture of how it should work. Implementing identity and access management in a practical and cost-effective way is another story. If your company has hundreds of resources and thousands of users, keeping track of them becomes an astronomical task. If you further open your systems to external parties such as business partners, suppliers, or customers, the problem grows exponentially.

This chapter focuses on the key components of identity and access management that are important for the auditors and that will enable a significant reduction in costs if appropriately implemented. The chapter begins with an architectural discussion about how to select an identity management solution in the most efficient and thorough way possible. Your identity management solution will become deeply ingrained into your infrastructure; if you select the wrong product, you will live with enormous pain for the foreseeable future or you will spend a small fortune on a "rip and replace" project.

The second half of the chapter addresses the ongoing operational components of identity and access management. Ultimately, identity and access management is an operational activity prefaced by an architectural implementation.

The Big Picture

Identity and access management encompasses a number of concepts, including password self-service, user access provisioning and deprovisioning, directory services, single sign-on, role-based and rule-based access control, and federated identity. Each of these components is briefly described below. This chapter will then focus on the components that are the most relevant to audit compliance and cost savings.

Password Self-Service

Password self-service is a technical functionality that allows users to reset their passwords by answering certain personal questions, rather than calling the help desk. The popular password self-service tools integrate into a number of commonly used systems and provide the user a self-registration function. The tool is configured to display a certain number of prewritten personal questions that a user must answer. Most tools offer the option to allow users to select a subset of the available questions—the ones that are most meaningful to them. Most tools also offer the option to allow users to create their own questions.

During the self-registration process, the user enters answers to the questions, which are stored securely for future use. When the user needs to reset his or her password, the tool randomly selects a specified number of the saved questions and requires the user to answer those questions. If the answers provided by the user match the answers provided by the user at the time of registration, the user is allowed to enter and confirm a new password. The tool then automatically sets that new password for the user on all systems with which it interfaces.

Most users can reset their password faster than they can reach a help desk representative; because password resets tend to be the single most frequent reason why users call the help desk, a significant cost savings can be achieved in reducing help desk staff if you can reduce the number of password-related calls. Password self-service offers the added benefit of synchronizing a user's password across multiple systems. This enables users to access more systems with just one password, reducing the likelihood that the user will write down his or her passwords or select an easily guessed password.

User Access Provisioning and Deprovisioning

User access provisioning and deprovisioning can be accomplished through a technical functionality whereby user IDs are created and permissions are granted automatically by a system, rather than by a person. The implementation and configuration of a user provisioning tool is highly complex, but if it is correctly done, it results in near-instantaneous provisioning (and deprovisioning) of user access. There are a number of advantages to implementing such a tool:

- Users receive their access immediately, avoiding the need or inclination to share accounts with others while they wait.
- Access is granted accurately every time, reducing the number of user complaints about incorrect implementation and eliminating audit findings around extraneous access that may have been inadvertently granted.
- Access is granted uniformly to specified groups of people, simplifying audit reviews.
- The tool can determine what access a user has, ensuring that terminations can be executed completely and accurately.
- Most tools come with a built-in or associated workflow module that allows users to submit requests that can be automatically provisioned if they are asking for preapproved access. If the request is not preapproved, it can be automatically routed to an approver and, upon approval, the provisioning will happen automatically.
- Automating a portion of user provisioning and deprovisioning can help reduce the user administration staff, resulting in a head-count savings.

There are also a number of challenges in implementing a provisioning tool, including:

- Not all tools can provision or deprovision. Some tools can only create a user ID, and perhaps partially provision the ID. Much of the provisioning process—and therefore the deprovisioning process—may remain manual. It is helpful to determine, roughly, how many times a person's access is expected to change in your organization in the course of the average person's career. Then consider that an ID is only created once on each system. If the average number of expected changes is just five (and it will be more at most companies) and you consider that provisioning an ID is much more time consuming than creating the ID, a tool that can only create IDs is adding very little value.
- None of the current tools on the market is compatible with every system. This is impossible. The top vendors do their best to interface "out of the box" with the major systems used in the marketplace, such as Windows, various versions of UNIX and Linux, certain mainframes, Oracle/PeopleSoft, SAP, the top Directory vendors, and so on. Most of the vendors provide software development toolkits (SDKs), application programming interfaces (APIs), or other similar functionality that allow you to build custom interfaces to systems that they do not support directly. If your company has a lot of home-grown or legacy applications, you may end up doing a lot of development work or employ the provisioning tool vendor's professional services to build all of the necessary interfaces at a high cost.
- Many of the tools are still agent based to some degree. Provisioning tools these days can be agent based or agentless. "Agent based" means that an agent (a piece of code) resides on the target system. The tool interacts with that agent, which then executes commands on the target. "Agentless" means that the tool interacts directly with the target system through a compatible protocol, without the need of an installed agent. Many tools are still at least partially agent based and some are as yet entirely agent based. If yours is a large and dynamic company, you may find it difficult to implement an agent-based solution. Consider that you would need to deploy an agent to each one of your hundreds or thousands of devices, first testing that the agent does not interfere with the operation of those devices. Also, consider that each time you need to upgrade a device, you will need to ensure that the agent remains compatible. This must be weighed against

a potential loss in functionality with a comparable agentless tool. In some cases, agentless tools cannot provision to the level of detail that an agent-based tool can, although that is not true of all tools. Finally, some provisioning vendors may charge you on a per-agent or per-seat basis, which adds administrative complexity and fluctuating costs due to the licensing true-up processes.

■ Provisioning tools rely on an accurate system of record. Whether this is your Human Resources (HR) system directly or a directory that pulls data from HR, if key user data is not available to the tool, it will not function.

■ Provisioning tools are only as good as the information they execute. Interfacing with target systems is only half the problem. Even if you can get the provisioning tool to communicate with all of your key systems, it still needs to know what to "say" to those systems. Some provisioning tool vendors have come up with clever tools and processes to help you more quickly determine what access everyone needs so that you can input that information into the tool and get it working. But at the end of the day, the tool will do what it is told and has no way of validating the accuracy of the access data you have input. If you code the wrong access instructions into the tool or the instructions are outdated or not sufficiently granular, the tool will diligently grant all of your users the wrong permissions.

■ Not all provisioning tools can do introspection or reconciliation. Introspection is the tool's ability to "look" at an existing target system and determine the users that currently exist on that system and the access that they have been assigned. Reconciliation is the tool's ability to compare what exists on the target system with what should be, according to its access programming, and do something about the differences. This should include creating reports, overriding the discrepancies on the target system, directly incorporating the discrepancies from the target system, or triggering approval workflows to validate the discrepancies before they are incorporated or overridden. Introspection and reconciliation are critical activities when a new system is brought under the management of a provisioning tool because these activities enable you to ensure that the system is "clean" from an access perspective; thus, it can be accurately managed going forward. If the tool cannot help you with these activities, although it may prevent additional violations from occurring, you may be stuck with manually trying to clean up potentially thousands of existing users to achieve a clean state.

In a perfect world, your provisioning tool will integrate with all of your platforms and applications, and it will accurately and granularly provision and deprovision users on a nearly instantaneous basis. You can then redeploy almost all of your user administrators, leaving just a few to manage access permission data on an ongoing basis to ensure that it remains accurate over time. Auditing of user access will be a snap: with the press of a few buttons, you will be able to generate reams of reports showing the auditors how everything is in perfect order—everyone has "least privilege" access, transferred users have all been accounted for and verified, and all terminated users have had their access revoked.

In the real world, your provisioning tool will:

- Integrate with a hopefully not too small subset of your platforms and applications out of the box
- Help you clean up existing user records through introspection and reconciliation
- Provision and deprovision accounts to a reasonable level of granularity

Some manual intervention is not out of the question, reducing the number of user administrators that you can redeploy and eliminating the likelihood that your audit reports will be perfect. You will also be faced with months' or years' worth of development activities (or the vendor's professional services) to build additional interfaces, and some may never be worth building. Nevertheless, even partial automation can be a tremendous help in reducing your administrative costs, facilitating your audits, and making your user community happier.

Directory Services

Much of identity and access management involves creating and maintaining a repository of users and their various attributes, such as user positions, job function information, password self-service information, and so on. These attributes are most commonly stored in one or more directories. The directory structure must be architected so that there is a clear hierarchy of information that flows in the right direction. Because authentication and authorization in an identity and access management solution depend on the integrity and availability of the directories, it is imperative that the architecture account for this.

Single Sign-On

Single sign-on is a technical functionality that allows a user to move from system to system or application to application without having to re-enter authentication credentials every time. There are several ways to implement this functionality. Two common ways are by relying heavily on the directory and constantly referring to it for authentication information or by implementing an authentication system such as Kerberos. Single sign-on may have audit and security implications if it is implemented insecurely. A password or credential that is compromised will equate to a breach of all systems or applications the user is authorized to access. If adequate security controls are implemented in the single sign-on solution, there will be no audit impact or any hard cost benefit to the organization. But there will be an enormous perception of benefit from the users. Users will be thrilled not to type in their password all the time or remember multiple passwords, and they will view this as a significant time savings (i.e., soft benefit).

Role-Based and Rule-Based Access Controls

Role-based and rule-based access controls are procedural concepts at the core of identity and access management; without their definitions any provisioning tool you implement will be useless. Role-based access control is the concept that all users with the same job function will have the same system access, and users with different job functions will have different system access. Access roles tend to be fixed and apply consistently to everyone within a particular job function. Rule-based access control is the concept that users with certain attributes are allowed or denied certain system access. Access rules tend to be dynamic and are applied circumstantially—for example, based on location, time of day, other privileges assigned, seniority, completion of certain training, or other criteria.

Especially at large companies that have many individuals in specialized functions, it is impractical to formulate roles for the entire company 100 percent. The goal of role basing is to create some generalizations that allow for easier management of users. However, in executing this role basing, some large companies find that they have as many as — or more — roles than they have users. This clearly becomes counterproductive. Therefore, as with anything else, role basing should be done pragmatically. The 80/20 rule applies well here: define the most common 80 percent of what people need as access roles to facilitate user provisioning and audit validation. Handle the remaining 20 percent with access rules or an approval workflow.

Once established, access roles and rules will make the lives of your user administrators much easier and will enable you to implement an automated provisioning solution effectively. It will also make it easier to generate clean user reports for the use of your auditors. However, establishing the roles and rules is an enormously painstaking and largely manual process, and you can expect a multi-person team to take months to complete it.

Federated Identity

Federated identity is the set of technologies and processes that enables a user to log in with the same user ID and password on the systems of multiple companies or entities. Think of it as a sort of global single sign-on. At the core of the federated identity model is a directory that correlates a user's credentials from multiple sources. That directory serves as the translator for the user so that he or she can use a single set of credentials while the directory pushes the relevant equivalent to the target system. Clearly, this points to a need for interorganizational interoperability, and today that is still a very tall order. However, as more and more systems begin to use industry standard protocols, federated identity will become increasingly manageable to implement.

Common uses for federated identity include:

- Employee benefits: Employees of your company can use their company network IDs and passwords to access their health insurance, retirement, and other benefits, despite the fact that the benefits information is maintained by the individual providers on their proprietary Web sites.
- Government interagency communications: Most governments in this world have numerous disparate agencies that provide services to their citizens. It will be much easier for citizens to make use of the online services offered by these agencies if they can have one ID and password to give them access to all services. This in turn would increase the use of online government services, thus reducing operating costs for the corresponding agencies.
- Electronic commerce: Many large retailers and manufacturers have hundreds or even thousands of suppliers and other business partners. Standardizing authentication between them would facilitate electronic commerce substantially.

Key Control Points

Three critical controls are embodied in identity and access management: properly managing new hires, controlling access for users who transfer, and promptly terminating access for users who have left the company. These components are further described in the following subsections.

Starting Off on the Right Foot—New Hires and the "Least Privilege" Principle

It is very important to ensure that access is appropriately granted to new users in your organization so that they do not exceed the "least privilege" principle from day one. This principle specifies that a user should only have as much access as minimally needed to perform his or her assigned job functions—nothing more. Initially, as new users are learning the job or in training, it is conceivable that they require even less access than they will ultimately have. Certain unionized functions base privileges on tenure: users must complete a certain number of hours of work to obtain additional authority on the system.

The challenge for most companies with new hires is that there are not adequately defined roles and rules dictating what access the new person should be granted. Some companies also struggle with the concept of authorization and approval. Should a user's manager approve his or her access or should that fall to the data owner? This must be determined strategically and is discussed later in this chapter.

Maintaining Control over Time—Managing Transfers and Segregation of Duties

Controlling access as individuals move through the organization is the most problematic area for most companies; this is where the most violations of segregation of duties occur. Segregation of duties is the concept that a person cannot perform two complementary job functions that could lead to the individual's ability to defraud the company. For example, someone who has functions in accounts payable should not also have functions in accounts receivable. Likewise, on the IT side, a system administrator charged with granting access to a system should not also be the one charged with approving that access.

Over time, a person who moves from position to position within the company could amass permissions that end up violating segregation of duties or the least-privilege principle. An important part of user management to ensure that old access is removed if no longer needed is the verification of access each time an individual transfers from one department to another, gets promoted, or otherwise makes a move within the company.

But how do you know when someone has transferred? Most companies struggle tremendously with this challenge. The problem is that most organizations do not manage job functions at the granularity level that could distinguish differences among all transferees. For example, if in your HR system a user's department is denoted as "Accounting," there is no way to determine from the HR record whether the user is part of the Accounts Payable team or the Accounts Receivable team. If the user transfers from the former to the latter, clearly an access change is needed, but a review of HR department changes will not identify this user as a transferee.

Even if you can identify that someone has transferred, there is the additional problem of identifying what access the individual previously had and what access is now needed. This is similar to the problem described earlier with new hires. Some policy-level decisions also need to be made on overlapping duties for a user who is in transition. Is it acceptable in your organization for someone to violate segregation of duties for a period of time while he or she transfers from the old position to the new one? If not, how will such transitions be handled? These concepts are also discussed later in the chapter.

Terminations—Is That Person Really Gone?

Promptly removing access when a user leaves the company is considered critical to the auditors. If someone is no longer employed, he or she should no longer have access—period. But the process of accurately terminating a user can be daunting if you are unsure when a user leaves the company, if it is unclear what access he or she had in his or her job function, or if you did not have a strong transfer process to help you with access cleanups through the course of that person's career. Additionally, in some scenarios the person's termination date is different from his or her last day of employment. Nevertheless, an audit finding in the area of terminations is more serious than an audit finding in any other area of user management; whereas a small number of exceptions is acceptable in other areas, in the area of terminations it really is not. Therefore, you have two choices: mount a very serious effort to clean up terminations and tighten your processes or implement additional "mitigating" controls. Both options are discussed later in this chapter.

Implementation Problems and Pitfalls

Let us be very clear: any program related to identity and access management belongs under the ownership of the information security department—not the IT engineers, not the IT architects, not HR, not the directory services team. User management is inherently a security function and must therefore be driven by the security strategy. However, an identity and access management solution truly touches every system and every user in the enterprise. Therefore, collaboration and participation will be required from most or all other IT teams, HR, and most or all business units.

It will therefore be crucial to obtain buy-in and representation from a very large audience. In particular, participation is needed from other departments to get a clear and detailed understanding of how user management works today, to help you determine what needs to happen to streamline it. You also need to ensure that you select a solution that will effectively interoperate with the rest of your infrastructure because the technology components of a user management system will be embedded so deeply into your company's architecture.

The following subsections discuss some considerations and problems in implementing a user management solution.

Multiple-User Stores

Many companies, whether through the process of acquisition or as a result of being decentralized regionally, have more than one HR system. Even worse, a lot of companies do not have a centralized repository (or any repository, really) for keeping track of nonemployees such as temps and contractors. As a result, it is very difficult to determine accurately what has happened to a user. For example, most companies with two or more HR systems handle users that transfer between systems as a termination in the old system and a new hire in the new system. From an access perspective, that user should not be terminated, although his or her privileges may need to change. Therefore, if you rely on reports from your HR systems to inform you about who has left the company, and you are unable to correlate a termination in one system with a new hire in another, you may inappropriately terminate a valid user. Conversely, if you have no accurate way of tracking the comings and goings of your nonemployee users, you could be left with active IDs that have not had valid owners for a very long time.

Even if you do have several accurate stores, correlation could still be a challenge and will always leave room for error in an area where error is not well tolerated. Although it is outside the scope of an identity and access management program per se, it is strongly recommended that, as part of this effort, you consider consolidating your user stores into (ideally) one, or at most two (one for employees, one for nonemployees). This will ensure the most accurate view of information and will also make it easier to synchronize that information with other relevant sources, such as your directory and your provisioning tool. If you need to maintain users manually for a while longer, it will save your team a lot of time and effort in trying to correlate information and research the exact status of users so they can go about the job of simply keeping accounts clean.

Clearly, the effort to consolidate HR databases or create nonemployee repositories is a significant undertaking that must have the buy-in of the HR department and executive management. Information security can add value to this initiative by raising it as a requirement. Many HR organizations would like to undertake projects of this nature, but have not had sufficient reason to justify the budget and resources required. By throwing the information security hat into the ring and demonstrating how database consolidation and nonemployee tracking can reduce the costs of implementing an identity and access management system—as well as make the company more compliant for audit purposes—you may be able to help HR tip the scales in its favor and get funding approved.

Inadequate User Information

Whether your HR stores are consolidated or distributed, you may also have the additional problem of inadequate or inaccurate user information. Inadequate information really stems from the use of an HR system versus the needs of a user management program. From an HR perspective, it is sufficient to know a person's grade, job title, department, and manager to train and pay him or her. From a user management perspective, that manager could lead several functions and, even though the people under him or her have the same HR title, they may actually require different system permissions. Also, HR systems typically do not store user IDs because HR uses other identifiers such as employee number or Social Security number. This can cause problems for users with common names if there is a disconnect between their HR records and their user IDs.

For example, suppose a user is registered in the HR database as Thomas Smith, but his ID is created as tom.smith because he commonly goes by Tom. There is also a Tom Smith registered in the HR database. How do you determine to whom the ID tom.smith belongs? If you do not even have synchrony of user IDs across systems, the problem becomes even more dire. A company once had three users with last name Nguyen, and first initial H. The company's user ID format was first initial plus last name. A digit was appended at the end to avoid duplicates. The three users had IDs of hnguyen, hnguyen1, and hnguyen2. However, their IDs were not synchronized across systems, so they were each hnguyen in some places, hnguyen1 in other places, and hnguyen2 in still other places. It was impossible to distinguish who owned which ID on any given system without physically contacting the users and asking (and hoping they remembered accurately). To make matters worse, in the HR system, they all showed as being part of the same department (IT).

The conclusion that most companies reach is that the full user store must reside in the directory. The directory must be carefully architected to pull various bits of information from the appropriate system of record and be updated frequently enough to keep it accurate, while not bringing down the network or other systems. The directory should also have the authority to populate other systems with information from the system of record. For example, there are a variety of reasons why you might want to have the HR database store a user's ID. The directory could receive this information from the authoritative source (in this case, the user provisioning tool) and pass it on to the HR database. However, the directory would need to be configured never to populate user IDs from HR back into the user provisioning tool. Similarly, relevant user information from HR would be propagated to the user provisioning tool, to assist the tool in determining the appropriate role to assign or rules to apply.

The directory might be the authoritative source for still more information. Users may use the directory as an input mechanism to update their mobile phone number or home address. This information would get propagated to HR. For user management to be accurate and sufficiently granular, it is necessary for data from all of these sources, and possibly others, to be amassed in a single location and accessible on demand.

Similar to the HR consolidation project, architecting an adequate directory structure will require the buy-in and participation of your directory services department, as well as from HR and other groups that may be required to interface with the directory to provide or obtain information. A sound directory structure is the foundation of the identity and access management enterprise. If your directory is not clean, accurate, and thoroughly populated or if it is inadequately secured to protect this wealth of information, it does not make any sense to build additional components. Address the issues with your directory first.

Incorrect User Information

Incorrect information about a user is perhaps more damaging than lack of information. If you are basing access decisions for a user based on data from two years ago, you have a problem. This is again a mandatory cleanup project that is a prerequisite to the main identity and access management program and is the responsibility of the departments owning the systems of record. Maintaining accurate data is largely a procedural concern. Work with HR (or other departments as needed) to develop efficient processes for keeping data up to date. You may also need to retrain personnel in the use of certain system fields. If you need to transfer data from one system to another, the receiving system will expect a certain format. If someone has input data into that field that is not in the expected format, the data transfer will fail.

The problem of outdated information is of course much more prevalent in large companies, where it is not trivial to track the intradepartmental or even interdepartmental movements of individuals accurately. One effective solution to this is to build a workflow mechanism that is driven by HR. On a monthly basis an automated process could run against the HR databases and generate a listing of all users reporting to each manager. The managers could then be contacted via a workflow tool, presented with their list of employees, and asked to validate whether it is still accurate.

The manager should be able to respond directly within the tool with any changes that may have occurred. The manager's changes could be populated directly back into the HR database or could be submitted for manual review by an HR representative. An enforcement process could be implemented to ensure that managers perform this task within a certain number of days of receiving the notice; reports could be generated to executive management to demonstrate compliance (or lack thereof).

Selecting a Solution—Suite versus Best of Breed

As of the writing of this book, Thor Technologies has recently been acquired by Oracle, eliminating the last of the major provisioning tools as a point solution. All of the top provisioning, single sign-on, and Web access control (WAC) tools are now part of vendor suites. However, most vendors price the components of their products somewhat individually, so there is still an option to pick and choose various components from different vendors.

The debate between suite solution versus best-of-breed point solution has been raging in the identity and access management space for a while now. Despite the consolidation in the marketplace narrowing the choices down to pretty much just suites, the argument is still valid because it all boils down to cost. The theory is that if you purchase a suite of products, all of the components of your identity and access management solution will already interoperate, saving you time and money on integration. But, if all of the components in the suite do not adequately meet your requirements, the money you save (and more) on integration could end up being spent on customizing the product to meet your needs.

The solution to this conundrum will vary by company, but your decision must be clear and well substantiated. As previously mentioned, any identity and access management solution will be deeply embedded into your infrastructure and touch (theoretically) every system and user in your enterprise. The solutions are extremely expensive, and the amount of time and effort it takes to get them working is substantial. This is not a decision you want to botch or something you want to rip out half way into the implementation.

The best way to ensure that you are making the right decision is to establish a core team of technically savvy people to do a good, old-fashioned, consulting-style requirements analysis. The team of people should include:

- Your security architect, who should be familiar with identity and access management architectures, both generally, and as they apply to the specific vendors you wish to consider
- A member of your IT architecture or infrastructure team who can add additional input into integration considerations
- Someone from your user management team who can speak to the day-to-day pain points, issues, and needs as related to user provisioning and de-provisioning
- A member of your directory services team because the directory is a key integration point with the provisioning tool

Once you have your core team and they have had a chance to interview key stakeholders to get their input, they should create a detailed listing of requirements based on stakeholder input as well as their expertise. You may choose to break down your requirements into a variety of areas for readability. Some suggestions of areas to consider include:

- Functional. What must the tool be able to accomplish? For example, to what level of detail do you need the provisioning component to be able to provision or deprovision a user on a particular system? To which systems would you like to apply the WAC component? To what extent do you want single sign-on to work in your environment? What characteristics do you want the password self-service tool to possess?
- Integration. What are the key systems in your environment that the tool must support out of the box? What other important systems do you know no tool will support out of the box for which you expect to build custom interfaces? What are the industry standard protocols that you use in your environment and that you expect the tool to use?
- Architectural. Most vendors run their suite on a handful of platforms. For example, they may run on Windows or AIX operating system and on Oracle or Sybase database. What combinations of operating system, database, directory, and other components would be acceptable to run in your environment?
- Compliance. What reports do you need the product to be able to produce? What are your reconciliation and introspection requirements? Do you expect the product to be "SOX certified"? If you are a government agency, do you expect the product to be able to handle mandatory access control (MAC) as well as discretionary access control (DAC)? Do you need the tool to have certification and accreditation (C&A) to a certain level (e.g., C2 or B1)?
- Stability. Do you have requirements in terms of the vendor company's size, whether it is publicly traded or private, investments, and length in business? Would you be terribly concerned if it got acquired by another company?
- Performance. What type of throughput does the product need to be able to sustain? What are your uptime requirements?
- Security. Because we are discussing the evaluation of a security solution, you might think that security is adequately built into the product. But that is not always the case. Be sure to list your security requirements in terms of encryption, authentication to the product, recoverability, and whatever else concerns you.

When you list each protocol, each system, and each functional requirement in part, you will end up with a list that is hundreds of line items long. It is not unusual for a detailed requirements document to exceed 100 pages. As a brainstorming exercise, ending up with lots of line items means that you have carefully considered your environment and your needs. But you cannot expect to evaluate products reasonably based on so many detailed requirements. Therefore, the next step is to prioritize your requirements on a usable scale. The easiest scale to use is one to three. Any more than that and you introduce a level of granularity that makes the ranking process more arduous, without measurable value. The most common and useful way to set up your importance scale is as follows:

- 3 = Mandatory. This feature is absolutely necessary for your environment. If a product does not have this feature, it is a show stopper and the product should no longer be considered.
- 2 = Desirable. This feature would greatly enhance the usability of the system or would otherwise significantly add value. If this one feature is missing, it would not be the end of the world, but if multiple features ranked 2 were missing, that could aggregate into a show stopper.
- 1 = Luxury. It would be nice if this feature were available, but chances are most products do not offer it and not having it does not present any substantial problem. Of course, vendors that offer this feature should get some bonus points for it.

Your importance ranking should not be done with any specific product in mind. Rather, it should be done with your environment in mind. Focus solely on what is most important and relevant to you in the context of your company. In terms of ranking realistically, you should have a handful of items ranked 3 and a handful ranked 1. Most items will be ranked 2.

Once you have completed your requirements-gathering and -ranking exercise, you are ready to compare the vendors to it. First, select the vendors you wish to assess. For this initial exercise, you may want to consider all vendors who have a product that would be adequate for your company's size and needs. You may want to make some preliminary decisions based on the reports from research companies such as Forrester, Burton Group, IDC, Gartner, or others. Once you have selected your initial list of vendors, have one of your core team members schedule a call with one of the vendor's engineers and run through the list of questions. At this point, you should not divulge what the requirements mean to you in terms of importance. Simply have the individual answer your questions to the degree necessary for you to provide a scoring. A useful scoring mechanism for vendor capability is:

■ 0 = This feature is not offered or the product cannot meet this requirement.
■ 1 = This requirement can be met with some customization.
■ 2 = This requirement can be met out of the box and only requires configuration to achieve.
■ If you are concerned about vendors scoring very similarly, you may choose to have a ranking of 3 = the product exceeds the specifications of this requirement. Basically, allow the vendor to earn "extra credit" if your expectations are exceeded.

Finally, for each vendor, generate the line-item scores and total score. The line-item score is simply the importance value times the capability value. For example, if you rank an item as having an importance of 3 (mandatory) and the vendor can meet that requirement (capability score 2), the line-item score would be 3 × 2 = 6. If you use the 0 to 2 capability scoring mechanism, 6 is the maximum score possible. If you allow the extra credit capability score of 3, 9 would be the maximum line-item score. Of course, 0 would be the minimum capability score possible. The vendor should not receive any credit for that which it cannot do.

After you have determined the line-item scores for each vendor, add them up to come up with a total vendor score. The vendor with the highest score is theoretically the most compatible with your environment. However, unless there is a very large and very clear discrepancy between the top two or three vendors, you may wish to do some further analysis here. Take a look and determine why one vendor scored better than another; is it because it was good across the board or because it got very high marks in just one area and mediocre marks everywhere else? Such a vendor may not be as beneficial for your long-term use as a vendor who did not score exceptionally well anywhere, but scored reasonably well across the board.

Irrespective of how variant the scores, it is imperative that you have your top choice and at least the runner-up come in and demonstrate their products in your environment. Take the top requirements that you documented and convert them into testing criteria and have the vendor demonstrate how those requirements are met. You may find that the vendor looks better on paper than in-house.

After you have done your paper-based assessment of prospective vendors and you have seen them perform live, you are ready to make the suite versus best-of-breed decision. If you have followed all of the steps outlined here, carefully documenting decisions that were made along the way and letting the requirements and not politics or personal preferences choose the product, chances are your selection will be the right one for your organization and you can implement with confidence knowing that you are doing the right thing and will not need to backtrack later. If, after a year or two, the requirements change drastically in a way that you could not have foreseen and someone questions your decision, you will have all of the evidence you need to demonstrate that, at the time, it was the best possible decision you could have made.

This section has been focused on the selection of an identity and access management solution. However, the methodology applies to any product selection and is a good way to ensure that you are making the right decision before issuing a purchase order.

Making User Management Operational in Its Current State

Most companies do not yet have a mature identity and access management system in place. Some have a partial implementation and others are just now tearing their hair out over what suite to select and how to implement it; still others are thinking that identity and access management is something they will want to do someday. Regardless of your current state, the reality is that you likely still have some, and possibly many, manual user management processes in your environment. If those processes are here to stay, they need to be as accurate and efficient as possible, to keep costs down and minimize mistakes that could be found by the auditors. Even if those processes are pending replacement with an automated solution, you likely still have an audit between you and the solution, and the cleaner the manual process is, the easier it will be to automate. Therefore, let us discuss how to ensure that your most scrutinized controls are as effective as they can be, taking into consideration the human factor. The rest of this chapter discusses how to be efficient for the sake of audit as well as for the sake of your business. After all, the auditors only breathe down your neck once a year, but end users do it daily.

Getting Off to the Right Start—Approvals

One of the key things that auditors will want to know is, "Was access approved?" For some companies, that alone is a problem. The even bigger challenge is yet to come: auditors are starting to look deeper, and "Was it approved?" is no longer adequate. They are now starting to look at "Who approved, and why is that the right person or group to approve?" Then the problem becomes much bigger, because in many organizations the person or group approving really is not appropriate—it is just better than nothing.

What about approvers whom you frequently bypass because they are slow to respond—or all of those emergency requests that may get by without any approval because it was an emergency? The auditors really do not like those situations. Maybe the right approver is approving, and the control is working just fine, but it is all done verbally, so you cannot prove that there is a control. This latter situation happens most frequently in the case of small applications where the approver is also the system administrator — a "no-no" for segregation of duties.

Remediating approvals is no small job, but once done can be fairly easily maintained. Also, the work you do in establishing this entire process will likely be reusable by other IT departments or even business groups across the company because just about every unit in the company must make requests of others and obtain approval for them. Thus, in your remediation efforts you will be adding value not only from a compliance and customer service perspective, but also by providing an effective and streamlined process template that everyone else can use. The following subsections describe a step-by-step approach to remediating the approvals process.

Step 1—Take Stock

First, identify all of your audit relevant applications and systems, being sure to include privileged access (such as administrator or superuser) to any of these as separate line items. Then identify whether you currently obtain approval or should obtain approval, who the approvers are, whether they are the right people for the job, and whether their approvals are documented.

You will also want to list possible synonyms for the systems to assist your auditors. Especially if the auditors obtained your company's list of critical applications from the business, this could save you some time and unnecessary work. It is not unusual for IT departments to use a different nomenclature for applications and systems than do business people.

If the auditors are looking for business terminology, but your approvals have the IT equivalent, the auditors may conclude that you have not provided adequate evidence when in fact you have. By providing a mapping of business and IT terms as they relate to critical applications, you can ensure that the auditors understand the evidence provided, and you do not need to respond to a lot of irrelevant findings later.

Table 12.1 provides a template to help you get organized. The content row of the table provides a brief description of how to use each column in the table and why the information is important.

Step 2—Identify Gaps

If you are able to populate table 12.1 accurately, the gaps will speak for themselves, but you may need to do some validation. For example, it is possible that some of your critical applications will not need approval for users to access. If you answered "No" to the approval-required question, validate whether that is a legitimate answer. If it is, be sure to document why and post that document in your audit repository as described in chapter 7. If in fact approval should be required, that line item needs to be marked for remediation.

Similarly, if you have identified that the current approver does not have at least one backup, is not the right person or group to be doing the approval, or the approval is not recorded, this should be marked for remediation.

Step 3—Remediate the Processes

As we discussed in chapter 2, once you have identified all of your requirements, you should go through a prioritization exercise to ensure that you are positioning projects in the most effective way possible to meet business and audit demands and to ensure that you take full advantage of synergies between projects to avoid rework or duplication of effort. The remediation process for approvals is no different. You may find quite a long list of action items, so you will need to prioritize them somehow. Here is a suggested methodology:

- Identify the most "dangerous" items first—that is, the applications, systems, or privileges that could cause the most damage if abused. If any of these do not have rock-solid controls, they need to be remediated first. Many companies have gaps in the area of privileged access such as administrator, root, or DBA. A lot of companies

Table 12.1 Suggested Template for Accounting of Approvals Currently Obtained for Critical Application

System or Application Name	Applicable Synonyms	Approval Required?	Approval Obtained?	Approver (title or group)	Backup Approvers	Approver Appropriate?	Approval Recorded?
List the names of critical systems or applications here. You may wish to list privileged access (such as DBA, administrator, or root) as separate line items.	One common confusion with auditors is nomenclature. If they are looking for approval evidence for the accounts receivable application and you provide an approval for the AR25 group, they may surmise that you do not have the appropriate approval unless you make it clear that AR25 grants access to Accounts Receivable.	For critical applications, the answer will almost always be "yes."	This is where you document very honestly if approval is obtained. If the answer here is "sometimes" or "no" when the answer in the previous column was "yes," you need to fix the process.	What is the title of the individual or name of the group who can approve this type of access? It may be the user's manager or a business owner. It should not be an IT support group.	If the approver is an individual, you need to have at least one backup identified. This will help you provide better service to customers and avoid granting urgent access without approval because the approver is on vacation.	Are the current approvers appropriate to the role or are they just filling a gap? If the answer to the second part of the question is "no," you will need to identify a more appropriate individual or group to take on future approvals.	For some applications, you may have a perfectly appropriate approval process, but if the approvals are not documented anywhere, you will have a problem with the auditors. A "no" in this column indicates the need for a process change.

actually have very tight control over their privileged access, and only key individuals or teams receive privileged access. However, it is often the case that privileged access is a condition of employment and is granted automatically. For example, if you hire someone to be a Windows system administrator, he or she will be added to one or more of the Windows administrator groups when joining the team. But because this privilege is implied, there is no formal approval process; it is just granted by someone else on the team. For the purposes of audit, an approval trail needs to be created. This should be a relatively simple remediation. At a minimum, have someone submit an e-mail or simple form to the team manager asking permission to grant the new person access and have the manager reply with the approval. You can then store a copy of that e-mail as evidence.

■ Identify the "low-hanging fruit." The previous example also qualifies as low-hanging fruit. It would be fairly easy to implement a simple process to create evidence for a control that is already effective. Applications in which the approvers and control process are in place and you simply need to produce evidence should be prioritized among the first because you can easily cover a lot of ground in a short time. Another example of low-hanging fruit would be to identify backup approvers. This could be an individual's peer or supervisor. In most cases, the current approver could easily identify one or more backups; all you need to do is ask.

Once you have tackled the high-priority and easy remediations, work on the more complicated solutions. These would be applications that are totally managed by the business and about which you may know little or nothing from your IT vantage point. Another challenge is to find people to take ownership of being an approver if an approver currently does not exist, is not the right person or group to approve, or is the approver for too broad an area, necessitating peer approvers to increase granularity.

These more complicated solutions may need to be handled as miniprojects because you will need to interact heavily with one or more business units, and you may need to get executive management support to encourage people to accept the responsibility of being an approver. Be sure to create a training guide that can be distributed to new approvers so that they understand their responsibilities. It is very important for them to understand that if they "rubber stamp" approvals, they severely affect the security of critical systems, which could lead to audit findings. They also need to understand that your team is prohibited from granting access before they grant their approval, so if they dawdle, one or more users will be without access, and this could affect the business. It is also beneficial to provide periodic refresher training to approvers, reminding them of their responsibilities, to ensure that they do not become complacent.

Once you have completed your remediations, update table 12.1 with the final solution and post it to your audit repository so that the auditors have a clear record of your work and improvements. You may also want to consider posting versions of table 12.1 to demonstrate progress, especially if your remediation will not be complete in time for audit. It is also a good idea to post any work planning materials you have created, to demonstrate the remediation time line and show that you are relatively on track for a timely completion.

Step 4—Automate If Possible

If you are a large company, automation is especially critical if you ever hope to keep accurate track of all of these approvals. Automation will also help you in providing better customer service because a workflow tool would automatically route requests to approvers and implementers without human intervention. This could save you hours or even days on the end-to-end processing of an access request. Also, by automating, you will have a centralized repository that can be used for a variety of reporting:

- Users can investigate their requests to determine status, without bothering someone on your team to assist them.
- You can run monthly reports of what was requested and approved or rejected for contribution to your audit repository as described in chapter 7. This is a big step in creating a self-service environment for the auditors because they can select sample users from the user reports you have posted, and then they can look up approvals from the workflow reports.
- You will also be able to better track frequency of request types and durations for service delivery, which will help you improve your customer service.

Implementing automation of approvals and therefore of user access requests is no small matter. This will be a fairly large and involved process. You will need to decide between building your tool in-house or buying a product that is available in the marketplace. This decision will depend on the size of your company, the number and complexity of your requests, and the amount of time you have to implement the new tool before it becomes an audit finding or before your customers kill you. It will also depend on the internal resources that you have available to do development work and what the prospect is for adequate ongoing support of the tool. Realistically, unless your company's core competency is software development and you want to get into the workflow market, you will be better off evaluating the products on the marketplace and purchasing one that suits your needs.

When it comes to workflow for user management, there are three broad classes of products from which you can choose:

1. Built-in functionality in an identity and access management suite. Most of the large vendors provide a workflow component with their user provisioning product. The advantage of going with their built-in product is that it already may be included in the cost of the provisioning tool, and you will not need to deal with integration. The disadvantage is that many of the workflow tools that ship with user provisioning products are fairly limited in scope. Users will be able to request access and possibly hardware or software with that workflow, but nothing else. If you want to provide users with a single tool from which they can request anything they need, including telephone or cellular equipment, facilities services, and even technical support or supplies, you will want to forego the savings in integration in favor of a tool that will provide a better user experience.

2. Technical workflow tool. A number of products on the market are designed to be used as generic workflow products. They will support a variety of different kinds of workflows, from IT service requests to business interactions. The advantage is that they are highly robust and can handle even the most complex workflows, often graphically. The disadvantages are that you must build all of your workflows from scratch, possibly being offered a few templates and some guidance to assist you, and you would have an additional component in your environment to be integrated with the rest of your identity management solution.

3. Service catalog tool. A small number of products on the market are sold as service catalog tools. A service catalog is a listing of services that are typically provided by a particular business unit—in this case, IT. This line of tools, in addition to providing basic service catalogs in key IT areas out of the box, also tends to offer user-friendly Web interfaces and familiar shopping cart

style applications. The advantages are that you may be able to build your services more quickly because you would not be starting from scratch, and you would provide a very friendly experience for your users, potentially eliminating or at least decreasing a variety of status inquiries and the possibility of mis-submitting requests. The disadvantages are that you still have the integration problem, and this line of tools has a somewhat more lightweight workflow capability. It may not be able to handle the most complex workflows in your environment.

Ultimately, what you choose will depend on how customer focused you are, how far reaching you want the workflow tool to be, and how much you have to spend. Any one of the three solutions described here will provide you with the control and reporting you need to meet your audit requirements if you appropriately configure your new tool and accurately account for your critical applications and their approval requirements. Thus, the decision hinges on your other priorities and strategic vision.

If the business is interested in implementing an enterprisewide workflow tool that can be used ubiquitously, go with the technical workflow tool. If you need to have a greater customer service focus, want to make things easy for your end users, and ubiquity is not a requirement, consider a service catalog product. If speed of implementation is a top priority, and you have a solution for providing a single user front end for your access request system and other IT requests or are not concerned with providing a single user front end, select an identity and access management suite with a strong workflow component and use that directly.

Regardless of your decision, be sure to document your requirements and selection decisions and also create an architecture document of your new product that explains how the workflow functionality works, how it prevents requests from being implemented prior to being approved, and what security mechanisms are in place to protect the data store of approval information. All of this documentation should be posted to your audit repository so that the auditors have easy access to the information.

Keeping It Clean—Terminations

Keeping track of terminations can be a nightmare, especially if you have multiple data stores for users (multiple HR databases and/or disparate tracking mechanisms for nonemployees such as temps and contractors). As previously discussed, multiple data sources could, at best, cause inconvenience to your users if you accidentally terminate someone who is still active. At worst, you could end up with dozens, hundreds, and over time thousands of active accounts that belong to users who have long since left the company.

This is the worst violation of authorization from the auditor's point of view. It is one thing to have a user that may have amassed access over time through a series of inter- or intradepartmental transfers (discussed in the next section). That is not good. But if the person is still an employee in good standing, the risk is not as severe as giving people the possibility of access when they have been escorted out of the building, left unhappy, or took a job with one of your competitors.

This section describes strategies for tackling the terminations problem in terms of going forward and for conducting a cleanup of your existing accounts.

Enforce Technologically

The best controls are automated ones that require minimum or no human intervention. In the area of terminations, this is best accomplished by setting inactivity timeouts on all of your systems. For legacy systems that do not support this functionality natively, it can be relatively simple to create some scripts that will execute this task. An inactivity timeout is a configuration setting on most newer systems that allows you to establish how long an account can be inactive (i.e., not used) before it is automatically disabled or deleted. The system will regularly check all of its accounts, and if it encounters any that have exceeded the established threshold, it will take action.

How you set the threshold will depend on the systems, their use, and the data they contain. Clearly, systems with critical or particularly sensitive data will have a lower threshold. As part of your security policy or hardening standards, you should determine what your threshold criteria should be. Here are some additional considerations:

- Think about the frequency of use of the system or of particular accounts on the system. If the system (or account) is only used monthly, quarterly, or annually, you will need to address that in your threshold calculation.
- Determine the sensitivity of the data on the system. If the data is highly confidential or sensitive, you may want to have very low thresholds.

■ Keep your company's culture in mind. If a large number of your employees take long vacations (e.g., a month or more), you will need to account for this in your calculations. This will be especially relevant for companies that operate in certain European and South American countries, where it is not unusual for employees to take a four- to six-week summer vacation.

■ Typically, the threshold for deleting an account is set to double the threshold for disabling an account. For example, if you set the account to be disabled 30 days after the last login, you would set the account to be deleted automatically 60 days after the last login. This is just a guideline; the time difference should be such that it makes sense in your organization. For example, rather than accommodating infrequent systems use or long vacations, you may establish a policy that any account that has not been used for, say, two weeks will be disabled. If users only use the account on a monthly basis or take a month off, they should be prepared to call the help desk to have their accounts reactivated when they return. Of course, this tactic should be carefully reviewed with the help desk to ensure that its personnel can handle the potential increase in calls, and it should be well communicated to the users so that they do not get frustrated trying to log in on their first day back. This is a prime example of a situation in which security and usability are at odds with each other. You will need to balance this one judiciously.

■ Be careful with operating system accounts that facilitate application accounts. Many applications, especially older ones that have their own internal authentication, rely on the creation of an operating system account to function; however, the user is unaware of that account and does not ever use it. If you were to set inactivity timeouts at the operating system level in this situation, all of your legitimate users would lose their accounts.

■ Test carefully before implementing the account deletion feature. Especially when first implementing this feature on your systems, you may find a lot of accounts that will be disabled or deleted immediately. Be sure to take a backup first in case you missed a criterion and delete legitimate accounts. Once the process is established and people understand the control, the danger of eliminating accounts incorrectly should go away.

■ When you first implement the control, be sure to communicate thoroughly with the users of each system so that they know this is coming. Hopefully, you did your homework and you will not have a noticeable impact on users, but if you choose to implement a low inactivity threshold, users need to know.

Engage HR and Finance

Clearly, the technological implementation of inactivity timeouts, although extremely useful in preventing accounts from slipping through the cracks, has two major unacceptable limitations:

1. The account must be idle for weeks or possibly months before it is disabled.
2. On some systems, due to the way accounts are used (i.e., application that relies on existence of an operating system account that is never actually used), inactivity timeouts cannot be implemented.

Although implementing inactivity timeouts is strongly recommended and can help strengthen the control, it is inadequate. You also need a real-time termination process that takes effect when a user announces that he or she will be leaving or is fired. But, as previously mentioned, if multiple sources of record exist for a user's "existence" at a company, determining who is really gone can be quite a challenge. The best way to fix this is to engage HR for employees and possibly Finance for nonemployees.

When questions arise about an employee, no one knows the status better than HR. Hopefully, HR will also know about nonemployees, but if hiring temps and contractors is a departmental function at your company, turn to your Finance team. They are the ones that must pay these people, so they should know whether the person is still employed. They will also know what may be happening with the person next. For example, is an employee really leaving the company or just moving to a different division that is on another HR system? Maybe the individual is staying on as a contractor? Likewise, a contractor may get hired as an employee. In these situations, although there has been a "termination" from the point of view of HR or Finance, the user may still need access, so the ID should not be revoked.

By engaging HR and Finance to be the initiators of all termination requests and also tying into their existing process to avoid duplicating their current effort, you can ensure that you are consistently notified of terminations, thereby largely avoiding the question "Is this person really gone?" HR and Finance should already have forms that they fill out, hopefully electronically, when a resource leaves. You may need to work with them to add some information to their existing forms or to help them automate the forms so that you can share their data. For example, their current form may not include information about whether the user is staying on in some other capacity, and you would need to know this information.

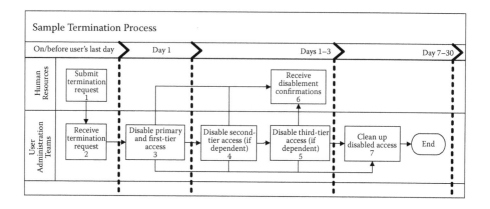

Figure 12.1 Sample termination process. This is a simple but efficient way to document a termination process. Please note that your specific process should be much more detailed. For example, you may want to have a swim lane for each of your user administration teams, or by platform, instead of lumping them into one. It is suggested that basic access such as network, connectivity, e-mail, and remote access be revoked within 24 hours of the user's departure from the company. That is also a good time to start revoking other access that does not depend on anything. Tasks 4 and 5 are optional and would only be needed if some disablement activities depended on others. If there are dependent tasks, it is recommended that they be completed within one to three days of the user's departure. This process assumes that it is possible to disable access rather than to delete it directly. Task 7, representing the action of deleting previously disabled access, should be done one week to one month after the disablement tasks were completed. The exact time lines for each of the tasks should be determined and documented in your security policies.

Figure 12.1 depicts a suggested termination process. Three disablement tasks are depicted because in some systems there may be a dependency between tiers of the architecture. For example, it may be necessary to clean up access at the application layer first, before removing access at the database or operating system layer. There is also some variability in the terminology between disable and remove because this is a generic example. Some systems, especially older or homegrown ones, may not offer the option of disabling an account—it is active or it does not exist. If that is the case, you will have no choice but to delete the account.

If there is an option to disable, you should consider disabling the account first and then deleting it after a certain time, such as one to two weeks. That way, if there was any mistake, you can easily re-enable the user rather than re-create accounts. If you can compensate for removing access on systems without a disable option by disabling the account in other areas so that the user could not get to the target system, you may want to leave an account active for the period of time that other accounts are in disabled status and perform the delete at the same time with the others.

When you develop your termination process, you will need to consider:

- Will you directly delete or disable first?
- If disable then delete, how long will you allow accounts to remain in disabled status prior to being cleaned up?
- If there are systems without a disable feature, do you want to delete immediately or leave the accounts active during the disablement period of other access?

These are policy decisions that should be documented. Your decision may depend in part on the type of termination: voluntary versus involuntary. You may wish to consult with your auditors also to get their input into this decision.

Table 12.2 provides the detail behind each step in the flow in figure 12.1.

Automate If Possible

Similar to approvals, terminations are a good thing to automate with a workflow tool. This will ensure that the request gets to access administrators quickly and the completion of tasks will be tracked centrally so that you can provide evidence to the auditors. It will also be important to enforce the service level agreements (SLAs) on executing account disablement or deletion. Figure 12.1 suggests that most of the work be done within 24 hours of the user's departure. Any follow-on cleanup activities may take weeks to complete, depending on how you set up your policy. It is not difficult in a manual situation to overlook the follow-on cleanup tasks, whereas with an automated tool, the task would be generated to the administrators when it is time for them to act.

In addition to ensuring that administrators are receiving and completing the disablement and deletion tasks, the auditors will want to see that the tasks were completed in the time specified in your policy. Therefore, if you specify that initial terminations must be completed within 24 hours, the auditors will want to see reports demonstrating that all initial termination tasks are completed within 24 hours of receipt.

Table 12.2 Process Flow Description Table for Figure 12.1

Step	Description	Responsibility	Deliverables
1.	Submit termination request: An HR representative completes a request form to terminate the user's access. Note: The form must be submitted on or before the user's last day of work.	HR	Completed request
2.	Receive termination request: User administration teams receive the termination request. Note: If you are doing this manually, the form may be received via e-mail or even by fax, although this is not recommended. Ideally, you have a workflow tool that will automatically route the request to the appropriate parties.	User administration teams	None
3.	Disable primary and first-tier access: Disable primary access such as network, e-mail, and remote capabilities. Disable all other access that has no dependency.	User administration teams	Disabled accounts
4.	Disable second-tier access: Disable any access that depends on first-tier access being already disabled. Note: This task may not be applicable in some environments.	User administration teams	Disabled accounts
5.	Disable third-tier access: Disable any access that depends on second-tier access being already disabled. Note: This task may not be applicable in some environments.	User administration teams	Disabled accounts

| 6. | Receive disablement confirmations: When access is disabled, the administrator should notify the HR representative and any other interested parties that the task has been completed. Note: In a manual environment, notice may take the form of an e-mail, fax (not recommended), or phone call (not recommended because cannot be audited). If a workflow tool is used, simply marking the task complete and entering a comment if appropriate would suffice. The HR representative would then be able to access the tool to view status or receive notification e-mails as tasks are completed. | User administration teams | Notice of action |
| 7. | Clean up disabled access: After the specified wait period, disabled accounts should be permanently deleted from the system. | User administration teams | Deleted accounts |

Distribute Widely

Without an established identity and access management solution, the reality is that most companies do not know what access a user has unless someone logs into every single system and checks. You could make some educated guesses, but if you also do not have a well-defined transfer process (described later in this chapter), your guesses based on a user's current access might lead you to overlook access that he or she may have had years ago that is still active. The inactivity timeouts will help substantially with this, but because we have already determined that that control also has limitations, it is important to distribute the termination notice widely.

Realistically, it takes an administrator just a moment to check for the existence of a user on a system. If the user does not exist, it is not a significant time drain. If the user does exist, it is important to handle the termination on that system. By engaging so many other teams and adding extra work to their resources, you may also gain valuable support for your efforts on selling the implementation of an identity and access management solution, which would significantly reduce or eliminate the need for so many teams to engage in manual termination activities.

Managing the User's Life Cycle—Transfers

Transfers are the most challenging of the three key access controls to manage because you must know when a user has transferred, as well as what access that user had in the old role and what is needed in the new role. Getting new access is never a problem; users will request what they need and complain if they are missing something. But identifying and removing access that is no longer needed is a challenge, and aggregate access can lead to significant audit findings, including segregation of duties violations.

To manage transfers, you need to have an identity and access management solution that is well integrated into your environment, with your access roles and rules fairly granularly defined. In the absence of that, unless you are a small company with a stable workforce and a relatively low number of systems, you must do a lot of work to manage transfers. This section attempts to provide some suggestions on how to manage transfers most efficiently if they must be done manually. This is definitely an area in which you may want to sit down and have an honest conversation with your auditors and get some guidance on what they would consider reasonable in terms of meeting the control without hiring a department's worth of people simply to manage the transfer process.

Identifying Transferred Users

The first challenge is to identify users who may have transferred. In a multi-HR company, the difficulty is similar to the one described in the terminations section. The other problem is to identify the attributes in a person's HR record that may indicate that he or she has changed job functions. The following examples of attributes may be telling. Work with your HR department to determine how to interpret changes to these attributes and how you might combine attributes to eliminate false positives and false negatives:

■ Cost center
■ Department
■ Job code
■ Manager
■ Title
■ Promotion/demotion indicator
■ Tenure (this may be helpful if your workforce is unionized or if you base privilege on number of hours worked)
■ Indication of completion of training (if you base privilege on the confirmation that a particular course was taken and passed)

If you have long-term contractors who could periodically change job function, hopefully you have a method for tracking these individuals (refer to the terminations section for suggestions) and that method includes a way of identifying at least whether the contractor is reporting to a new manager. Discuss with HR, Finance, or any other organization that has control over the management of contractors about how you might identify important changes to a contractor's status.

Once you have determined who has transferred, you must devise a mechanism for managing that person's access such that any privileges that are no longer needed will be removed. Generally speaking, there are two ways to manage transfers manually. One is more security centric and less user friendly. This one is described in the next section. The second option, described in the following section, is more user friendly, but takes more effort to manage and could result in less accurate access cleanup. These are merely suggestions that are at relative opposite ends of the spectrum, to get you started. Depending on your capabilities, you could implement some reporting facilities to narrow down what access users have and make use of your workflow tool (if you have one) to obtain specific approval from the old and new managers to retain certain components of that access.

The important thing here is to keep it simple or push the implementation of an identity and access management system. You could build an identity and access management solution from scratch to manage transfers if you get carried away. If you are going down that path, you might as well save some time and effort and evaluate a "tried and true" product that is available on the market.

Manually Managing Transfers—Option 1

In this option, you take the security-centric approach. Identify your critical systems and create a partial-termination process whereby the user's existing access to critical systems is disabled (or if disablement is not an option, deleted). If the user needs any portion of that access in the new position, he or she will need to submit a formal request and be approved to have that access reinstated. The advantage to this method, of course, is that you are less likely to miss any old access that should be removed. The disadvantage is inconvenience to the user, which can be significant. It could also be an inconvenience to the user administrators if they must disable access and then re-enable it, or worse, delete the access and need to recreate it.

If you are going to implement a process of this nature, you need to define it carefully in your policy and also consider how you will handle transitions. It is not unusual for users to require access from their old job function for a period of time after their official transfer date because they may still provide support to the old manager, need to train their replacement, or learn their new job before leaving the old one. Many times, this does not create any significant conflict and can be accommodated without much difficulty. But there are times when the overlapping access has segregation-of-duties implications. You need to define in your policy if this is ever acceptable or if there will be an expectation that segregation of duties will not be violated as a result of job transfers.

You also need to communicate this process very clearly and frequently to the company so that everyone is clear on the policy and how transfers will be handled. By preparing users that their access will be removed, you can avoid complaints and potentially even have them preempt the incorrect access removals by submitting a request in a timely fashion.

Figure 12.2 generically depicts how this process might work. The details are provided in table 12.3.

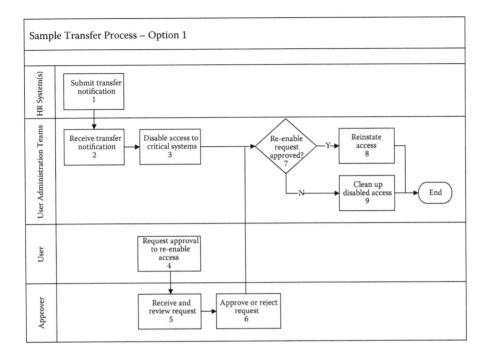

Figure 12.2 Sample transfer process: option 1. This process depicts the scenario in which a user's existing access to critical systems is automatically revoked and the user must request reinstatement. The decision to use this method would need to be documented in your policy and communicated to the user community. You would also need to specify how long administrators should wait for an approved reinstatement request before proceeding with the cleanup of disabled access.

Manually Managing Transfers—Option 2

This option is much more user friendly but takes additional effort to manage and could result in users somewhat exceeding their authorization. In this option, whenever you identify that a user has transferred, you contact the previous and new managers and have them provide input into what the user requires. Of course, this must be automated unless your user population is extremely small. Again, a workflow tool would be extremely helpful in this regard. The managers would each respond with a list of access needed. Anything not on the list could be removed. This would also give the managers the opportunity to address the transition time frame so that access is not revoked prematurely.

Table 12.3 Process Flow Description Table for Figure 12.2

Step	Description	Responsibility	Deliverables
1.	Submit transfer notification: An automated report should be generated on a policy-specified basis from each HR system. Note: The recommended frequency for this is weekly.	Human Resources system	Notification
2.	Receive transfer notification: User administration teams receive the transfer notification. Note: The report may be delivered to the information security team, and then it would be their responsibility to distribute as needed. Otherwise, the report could be delivered to a centralized location and all affected administration teams could be notified that the report is available. The latter is the recommended approach.	User administration teams	None
3.	Disable access to critical systems: Disable access to critical systems until it is determined that the user is authorized to retain access to those systems. Disable second- and third-tier access as needed. Note: You will need to determine the critical systems. Basic access such as e-mail should not be disabled.	User administration teams	Disabled accounts
4.	Request approval to reenable access: Upon noticing loss of access, user requests approval for a temporary extension or permanent access.	User	Completed request
5.	Receive and review request: Receive request from user and review it for business need. Consider segregation-of-duties implications. Indicate a time limit if there should be one and the user did not specify one. Contact the user and ask questions if needed.	Approver	None

		Approver	
6.	Approve or reject request: Make and submit a decision.	Approver	Approve or reject decision formally documented
7.	Re-enable request approved? Determine whether a request was submitted to reinstate access and whether it was approved. If it was approved, proceed to step 8. If it was rejected, proceed to step 9. Note: You should dictate in your policy how long a transferred user's access remains in disabled status before it is deleted. Because in this scenario the user is not notified of the pending removal, it is recommended that at least one to two weeks be allowed to elapse, giving the user time to submit a request and obtain approval.	User administration teams	None
8.	Reinstate access: If approval was granted to reinstate access, reinstate all access for which approval was granted.	User administration teams	Access is reinstated in all approved locations
9.	Clean up disabled access: If approval to reinstate access was denied, proceed with the cleanup of disabled access.	User administration teams	Disabled access is deleted

The advantage of this method is that users are much less likely to be affected negatively, and user administrators need only act once instead of potentially twice. The disadvantage is that the list provided by the managers could be longer than necessary, so the user would end up keeping more access than he or she really needs. Also, you must manage responses. If managers do not reply, you must contact them and remind them. You will need an enforcement process, and you will need to spend additional time on enforcement.

Figure 12.3 generically depicts how this process might work. The details are provided in table 12.4.

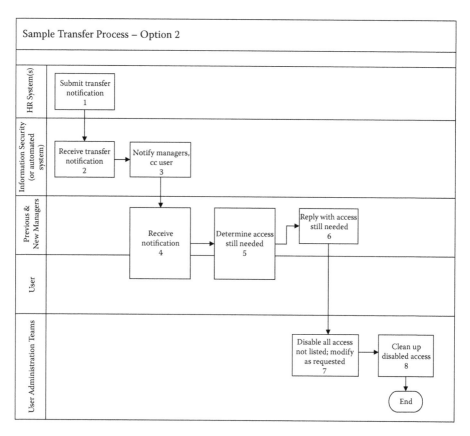

Figure 12.3   Sample transfer process: option 2. This process depicts the scenario in which a user's previous and new managers are contacted and asked for input into what access should be retained. The decision to use this method would need to be documented in your policy and communicated to the user community. You would also need to specify the time frame in which you expect the managers to respond and an escalation process for dealing with nonresponsive managers.

Table 12.4   Process Flow Description Table for Figure 12.3

Step	Description	Responsibility	Deliverables
1.	Submit transfer notification: An automated report should be generated on a policy-specified basis from each HR system. Note: The recommended frequency for this is weekly.	HR system	Notification
2.	Receive transfer notification: Information security teams receive the transfer notification. Note: The report may be delivered to the information security team, and then it would be their responsibility to distribute as needed. Otherwise, the report could be delivered to a centralized location and the information security team could be notified that the report is available. The latter is the recommended approach.	Information security	None
3.	Notify managers, cc user: Determine the previous and new managers. Notify them via the official vehicle that they must act or the user will lose all current access to critical systems. Carbon copy the user so he or she is aware of the action that needs to be taken. It is in the user's best interest for his or her manager to respond in a timely fashion so that the user can be instrumental in ensuring compliance. Note: Ideally, you have a workflow tool that can be used to trigger a task to the managers. Otherwise, e-mail or some other written notification should be used. In the latter situation, be sure to design a standard template for the notification.	Information security	Formal notification to managers that action is required
4.	Receive notification: User's prior and current managers, as well as the user, receive the transfer notification.	User's previous and new managers; user	None

Table 12.4 (Continued) Process Flow Description Table for Figure 12.3

Step	Description	Responsibility	Deliverables
5.	Determine access still needed: The managers should meet with the user (together or separately) to determine what access from the previous position should be retained.	User's previous and new managers (primary); user (secondary)	Decision on access that will be retained
6.	Reply with access still needed: Managers reply via formal channel (workflow tool, e-mail, etc.) with a listing of what access is still needed, if any. Managers should also indicate whether any current permissions should be changed. Note 1: For efficiency, if the response is via e-mail, if possible, the managers should reply to information security and the user administrators to prevent information security from being the middleman and having to forward the request. Note 2: You may also want to route the needed access to the data owner for re-approval. This is a question to bring up with your auditors.	User's previous and new managers	Formal reply
7.	Disable all access not listed; modify as requested: Administrators should disable all access that is not listed by the managers as still needed. If any requests for changes were made, administrators should address these as well.	User administration teams	None
8.	Clean up disabled access: Proceed with the cleanup of disabled access after policy-specified waiting period has elapsed. Note: In this scenario, because the managers and user were involved and specified the needed access, the waiting period can be fairly small. There should still be a waiting period, however, in case the user and managers forgot to list something.	User administration teams	None

Mitigating Control—User Recertification

If any or all of your other controls (i.e., approvals, terminations, and transfers) are inadequate, it is advisable to implement user recertification as a mitigating control. User recertification is the process of reauthorizing access to all users on a critical system. You would need to define in your corporate security policy how frequently you would conduct a user recertification exercise; be sure to check with your business units because some might already be executing this task. In terms of frequency, annual action is the bare minimum. However, if the system is particularly critical or your other controls have significant weaknesses, the auditors may find annual action to be inadequate.

The process of user recertification is quite simple:

1. Generate a report of users from the systems you wish to recertify and the permissions that the users have on those systems.
2. Identify appropriate reviewers for each system (you may already know this information from setting up your approval process).
3. Have the approvers review their respective reports and note any changes that need to be made—namely, change access or remove access.
4. Make the changes as specified by the reviewer. If a user complains about the change, he or she should obtain approval from the reviewer to have access reinstated.

Although the process is simple, the implementation can be enormously tedious for a number of reasons, including:

- Whether a user truly has access to an application can depend on having access in multiple places—for example, at the operating system, database, and application levels. You may need to generate cross-system reports to get an accurate picture of who has what.
- For large applications, the user list may be thousands or even tens of thousands of lines long. This can be overwhelming to a reviewer, who may then be reluctant to participate. Even if he or she willingly participates, it is more likely that rows will be missed and mistakes made. It will also take a long time to conduct a review—possibly a month or longer.
- Also with large applications, there may be many reviewers— possibly one per department. This will take more tracking and coordination for your resources.

■ Some applications may be used companywide, and there may not be a central or even department-level approval. If that is the case, you may need to track down the current managers of every user in a report and get them to reply as to whether or not the user is still approved for access.

User recertification can be a full-time job for one or more resources throughout the year, especially in larger companies with lots of systems and users. The most cost-effective way to deal with user recertification is to lock down approvals, terminations, and transfers, thus eliminating the need for recertification. But if it must be done, here are some suggestions on how to be most efficient. Most will now sound familiar to you because these concepts have been mentioned throughout the book:

■ Create a master catalog. List all of the systems you need to recertify, potential alternate names for those systems, all of the locations for which a user ID is created to grant user access to that particular system, the generator of the report, the reviewer of the report, and the expected size of the report. Some of this information you may already have if you have created and populated something similar to table 12.1.

■ Create a standard for your user reports. Each system will present data somewhat differently, but you will need some basic information on each report, such as full name, user ID, permissions, location (department, division, or whatever other physical indicator makes sense for that particular system), and a reviewer response column. You may want to engage your reviewers in the creation of the report format to ensure that you come up with something acceptable to them. You will also want to discuss the file type of the report. Spreadsheet format tends to work well if you are going the fully manual route. If you have some skilled Web developers, you may want to create a Web-based repository by which reviewers can view their reports online and respond directly on the Web site.

■ Create a perpetual calendar. Work it out so that you are conducting recertification throughout the year and not all at once. Consider the size of the report (large reports should be sent out earlier in the year to give reviewers more time) and the workload of the reviewer. (If one reviewer is responsible for multiple systems, you may want to spread those out so that the reviewer is not deluged. Likewise, if the reviewer has a cyclical job in which he or she is very busy at a particular time of the year, schedule the recertification at another time.) This has the advantage of making the process more manageable for your resources and the reviewers, and well-defined schedules give the auditors comfort.

■ Create and distribute reviewer training materials. Be sure to outline the steps of the process and emphasize the importance of doing a thorough and timely review. Also instruct reviewers how they are to respond. In particular, they should be advised to place their full names and date of review on the report and make a comment for each line item—even if it is simply "no change." Leaving a row uncommented may lead the auditors to believe that the line item was not reviewed. When a comment is put in each row, the auditors gain comfort that the review was thorough.

■ Be consistent in your communications with user administrators. Rather than passing on entire reports after they have been reviewed, take the time to pull out the line items that require action and send only those to the administrators. Because the number of changes can be potentially large, by presenting administrators with only the data that pertains to them, you reduce the risk of implementation mistakes.

■ Communicate with your help desk. It is not unusual, especially in large companies, for reviewers to make mistakes and request the removal of access for a user that still legitimately needs it. Even at small companies reviewers can still make mistakes. Therefore, each time the administrators conduct a cleanup related to user recertification, be sure to notify the help desk and provide it with a list of users that were affected. This helps the user and the help desk representative because troubleshooting the problem will go much faster. It will also help with security if the help desk knows that the loss of access was due to a user recertification cleanup and approval is needed to reinstate access. Otherwise, the representative (if he or she has the capability) may just reinstate the access, weakening the effectiveness of the recertification process.

Monitor Solutions

In addition to your establishing a strong control, the auditors will want to see that you monitor that control on a regular basis. Monitoring is an easy way to help auditors gain comfort because there are no precise requirements for it. The auditors simply want to see that you are taking reasonable steps on a regular basis to verify that the control is functioning properly. Of course, as with anything else that is audit related, be sure to document your monitoring actions and post the documentation to your audit repository so that the auditors see your work and give you credit for your efforts.

Approvals

In the case of the approval control, any of the following could be used as monitoring tactics (and combining two or more is even better):

- Select a sample of critical applications each month and select a few users that have been added to the system. Then validate that there was a request associated with that access and that the proper approval was obtained prior to implementation. If you set up your audit repository correctly as described in chapter 7, all of the data should be at your disposal for review. This is a more involved monitoring mechanism, but should be very similar to the way your auditors will conduct their audit. By doing your microaudit each month, you may be able to identify and repair weaknesses in your control before the auditors find them.
- Conduct regular training with approvers to ensure that they are diligent in their approvals and not simply "rubber stamping" each request that crosses their desks.
- Run a report of requests that have been approved by a subset of approvers and verify that the access requested is appropriate for the users in question.

Terminations

The easiest way to monitor terminations is to select a small sample of terminated users each month and manually validate that their access is disabled or deleted on all systems. If "all systems" is a lot, select a sample of systems to verify and change that sample each time you perform the monitoring task. If you use a workflow tool to distribute the tasks, you could also run reports showing the percentage of termination tasks that were completed on time. If that value is significantly less than 100 percent, take corrective actions before the auditors arrive.

Transfers

Of course, monitoring for the least straightforward control is least straightforward. If you choose to use option 1, you might choose a small sample of transferred users and demonstrate that their access on their previous position's systems no longer exists. If it does exist, you should validate that there is an approval to support it. If you choose to use option 2, you may wish to review a sample of responses from managers and validate that the transferred user only has access to systems that the managers listed. If you have a hybrid solution, you will need to devise a mechanism for monitoring that is conscientious and can be executed quickly. Monitoring should not take much time—it just needs to be done. Here, again, an automated workflow tool with reporting capabilities will make life much easier.

User Recertification

As time consuming as the process of user recertification is, the monitoring component is remarkably painless. For each report returned by a reviewer, select a small sample of users that were marked for a change or removal of access and have someone verify that the changes were made.

Segregation of Duties

To ensure segregation of duties, preferably the person that executes the monitoring should not be the one that executed the original cleanup. For small systems that may only have one user administrator, he or she should physically show you each user or run a report demonstrating the changes. This in effect makes you the person monitoring.

Dealing with Discrepancies

If any discrepancies are found in the course of monitoring, be sure to have them fixed. If discrepancies are found consistently, you may wish to adjust your process, re-educate the people responsible for executing the parts of the process that are causing problems, and, if needed, do a deeper validation. Monitoring is your opportunity to catch flaws in your controls before the auditors do, so take discrepancies seriously, especially if there are more than could be reasonably chalked up to human error on the part of the executors.

What about Nonuser Accounts?

Nonuser accounts, such as service accounts, training IDs, batch IDs, and the like, are another piece of the identity and access management puzzle that must be addressed. Unfortunately, there is no HR record for these sorts of "users." A repository must be created and a recertification process must be developed to review existing nonuser IDs to determine whether they are still in use or are being used for authorized or unauthorized purposes, and to identify a human owner that will take care of the ID going forward. The good news is that auditors are not at the point of reviewing such IDs yet. The bad news is that it likely will not take long for them to start digging. Most companies have an enormous mess in this area. The cleanup will be extremely painful because most nonuser IDs are not well documented; no one really knows what those IDs do and the impact if they are removed. The processes described in this chapter as they pertain to user IDs can be applied to nonuser IDs as well. We highly recommend that you start working on this now, rather than reacting to an audit finding later.

Summary

Identity and access management, although fairly easy to describe in terms of architecture and purpose, is enormously difficult to implement. The solution theoretically will touch every user and every technology in your organization. It is critical that you carefully design the solution and judiciously select a product; you can expect the implementation to take quite a while.

This chapter began by outlining a methodology for architecting your identity and access management solution. Then the focus shifted to managing the manual processes that you have today while, or until, you build an automated solution. Because access management is one of the highest visibility controls on the radar of the auditors, it is imperative to clean up your manual processes to avoid findings until the enterprise solution comes into existence. It is also important to remember that the final solution is not a silver bullet; clean manual processes now will not only facilitate the implementation of the automated solution, but also will continue to fill the gaps where the solution falls short.

Chapter 13

Cost-Effective Incident Response

Introduction

Businesses depend heavily on the availability of data networks to conduct commerce. A virus incident that takes down hundreds of workstations or servers for a day could cost a company millions of dollars in unproductive staff time, as well as the cost of IT and security staff working around the clock to get these systems back up. With the advent of sophisticated self-propagating threats, a computer security incident response team (CSIRT) has minutes, not hours, to respond to curb the impact of a virus or worm.

Significant costs are associated with every security breach, especially when customer confidential data is involved. Millions of dollars can be spent on notification, investigation, public relations, and legal fees when a security breach occurs. In extreme cases, some companies have ceased to exist due to the compromise of millions of nonpublic customer records. Harking back to chapter 1, a sound incident response strategy contributes to the departmental goals:

- Ensuring minimal downtime to business critical functions due to security incidents
- Ensuring minimal compromise to confidential data due to security incidents

Due to the high costs of breaches and virus outbreaks, your department's ability to respond quickly and effectively to security incidents will result in significant cost savings. If you detect and prevent a virus from spreading before it infects a considerable number of systems, you have directly reduced the price tag of that incident to your company. Similarly, if you detect and stop a hacker before he or she reaches millions of customer records on your production database, you have saved the company a substantial expense related to damage control, as well as the intangible but likely enormously high cost of a tainted reputation. The onus is on you to report these monetary benefits to your executive management so that they understand the benefit that your department has once again provided. Refer to chapter 8 for details.

Cost savings can also be gained by developing an efficient and effective incident response methodology. In this chapter, we will discuss the different components of the incident response process and how they will be implemented to curb security incidents successfully without breaking the bank.

The Price of Not Planning

When you are in the middle of an incident, it is too late to plan. Your disorganization and lack of protocol will result in the incident spiraling downward as you scramble to put disjointed pieces of your CSIRT into action. The absence of good planning is the bane of any incident response strategy, consequentially costing your company more in the resources needed to contain the event as well as the actual damage incurred. There is no excuse for not planning.

Planning for the CSIRT involves establishing and defining the following components, which are detailed in subsequent sections:

- CSIRT objectives
- A high-level process
- CSIRT membership
- Responsibilities and expectations of each CSIRT member
- Templates and procedures to be used by the CSIRT during an incident
- Assessment of incident discovery tools
- "Sandbox" security lab to study infected machines (if your budget permits)
- Forensics procedure (if your budget permits and your company intends to prosecute intruders)

Start with Objectives

The CSIRT has the responsibility of addressing a security incident when it occurs. Your CSIRT should have the following objectives:

- Quickly confirm or dispel whether a security incident occurred.
- Resolve the incident or elevate the severity as appropriate.
- Accumulate and convey accurate information to relevant parties to contain the incident.
- Minimize disruptions to business and network operations while trying to recover from the incident.
- Establish controls for proper retrieval and handling of evidence.
- Provide proper analysis and reporting to decision makers to address incident damage, root cause, and remediation efforts.

At a high level, you want a CSIRT to quickly identify, contain, and recover from an incident. From a postmortem standpoint, you want the CSIRT to identify root cause, provide proper accounting of the incident, and propose fixes to the vulnerability that was exploited.

Assembling the CSIRT

The CSIRT should not comprise only individuals from your department. The cost-conscious and operationally effective way of formulating a CSIRT is to assemble a collection of individuals from a variety of IT and possibly business teams who are engaged at different phases of an incident, depending on their need to know and expertise. However, your core CSIRT should be composed of technical members of the security department.

Essentially, the CSIRT is one team made up of the following groups:

- Frontline is the group that will most likely detect the incident first (typically the help desk or your monitoring crew).
- Initial response team (IRT) has security subject matter expertise to confirm a security incident (typically members of your department).
- Executive incident team (EIT) is made up of decision makers in the event of incidents that can seriously affect the company.
- Responders focus on getting the environment back to normal (typically your IT engineering and support groups).
- Investigators make up the group that focuses on identifying root cause and preventative measures (possibly third-party experts).

The CSIRT will also engage other departments and groups as appropriate, such as Human Resources (HR), Legal, and Public

Relations, but they are not part of the CSIRT per se. The representation of these key departments can be consolidated into the EIT.

The Big Picture

Before we dive into the details of each group and its corresponding function, let us look at a high-level process of an incident response framework, as depicted in figure 13.1 and detailed in table 13.1. Figure 13.1 depicts an important component of your CSIRT training and drills. Communicating the roles, responsibilities, and procedures of the CSIRT process is a key component of planning for an incident. Good planning will save you and your company a substantial amount of money in the form of quick recovery, lowered liability, and optimal use of resources to address the incident.

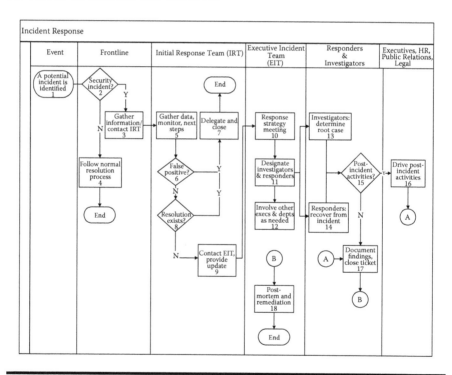

Figure 13.1 High-level incident response process. This figure demonstrates the course of action in resolving an incident, depending on its severity and the availability of a resolution. Note that this process is depicted with vertical swim lanes, instead of horizontal swim lanes as in other chapters. Choosing the direction of swim lanes is arbitrary, largely a condition of user preference. However, the "shape" of the flow may also make it more conducive to a horizontal or vertical direction.

Table 13.1   Process Flow Description Table for Figure 13.1

Step	Description	Responsibility	Deliverables
1.	A potential incident is identified: A user calls the help desk to report a problem with a computer or during monitoring someone notices an unusual event.	User or monitoring person	Call to help desk or report to information security
2.	Security incident? Frontline person accesses previously prepared decision tool and determines whether the symptoms reported are consistent with a security incident. If this is a security incident, proceed to step 3. If this is not a security incident, proceed to step 4.	Frontline personnel	Decision whether this is a security incident
3.	Gather information and contact IRT: Collect all available information (logs, notes taken during user interaction, etc.). Contact the incident response team (IRT) according to pre-established contact framework.	Frontline personnel	Information documented and packaged IRT contacted
4.	Follow normal resolution process: If this is not a security incident, the frontline person should resolve the problem in accordance with standard operating procedures for that type of problem.	Frontline personnel	Problem resolved according to SOP
5.	Gather data; monitor; next steps: Gather any other relevant data from other sources, such as system logs, other help desk reports, monitoring tool output, etc. Determine the extra monitoring to be enabled and enable it. Determine the next steps based on the evaluation of the data available so far.	IRT	Information documented and packaged Additional monitoring enabled Next steps determined and documented

(*continued*)

Table 13.1 (Continued) Process Flow Description Table for Figure 13.1

Step	Description	Responsibility	Deliverables
6.	False positive? Is there a security incident or was this situation a false positive? If yes (false positive), proceed to step 7. If no (security incident), proceed to step 8.	IRT	Decision made whether incident was legitimate or false positive
7.	Delegate and close: False-positive events should be studied and rectified to prevent future occurrences. Delegate false-positive incidents to someone for analysis and tuning of procedures, decision tools, or monitoring tools.	IRT	Event assigned to appropriate party for analysis and resolution
8.	Resolution exists? Is this a simple incident that is easily resolved? If yes, proceed to step 7. If no, proceed to step 9.	IRT	Resolution complexity determined
9.	Contact EIT, provide update: Contact the members of the executive incident team (EIT) to notify them that an incident has occurred. Provide a prereading update for them with information available so far, such as nature of the incident, when it started, how many systems or users are affected, potential solutions, etc. Set up a conference room and a dial-in number for the meeting with the EIT.	IRT	EIT contacted Prereading materials provided to EIT Meeting arrangements made
10.	Response strategy meeting: Conduct a meeting to determine the strategy for responding to the incident, considering impact to the business from downtime as well as image perspectives. Document decisions.	EIT	Meeting held Response strategy determined and documented

Table 13.1 (Continued)   Process Flow Description Table for Figure 13.1

Step	Description	Responsibility	Deliverables
11.	Designate investigators and responders: Determine appropriate individuals to investigate the incident and to respond to the incident. Document decisions and notify participants.	EIT	Investigators identified and notified Responders identified and notified
12.	Involve other executives and departments as needed: If the incident has the potential to cause significant downtime or to have an impact on the company's reputation, it is advisable to involve any or all of the following: other senior executives, HR, public relations, corporate communications, and legal.	EIT	Other executives and departments identified and notified
13.	Investigators: determine root cause: Investigators conduct their investigation in accordance with pre-established procedures, taking into consideration the desire to prosecute (or lack thereof). All findings are documented using pre-established templates. This step is executed in parallel with step 14.	Investigators	Documented findings
14.	Responders: recover from incident: Execute necessary steps to recover from incident and bring systems back online in a normal state. This step is executed in parallel with step 13.	Responders	Systems back to normal
15.	Postincident activities? Does anything need to be done after the incident is resolved, such as notifying customers, retraining employees, etc.? This does not include the postmortem activity, which is always executed. If yes, proceed to step 16. If no, proceed to step 17.	Responders	Systems back to normal

(continued)

Table 13.1 (Continued) Process Flow Description Table for Figure 13.1

Step	Description	Responsibility	Deliverables
16.	Drive postincident activities: The appropriate individual or group should do what is needed, such as communicating with the media, notifying customers, developing training for employees, communicating internally, taking disciplinary action, etc. Upon completion, proceed to step 17.	Other executives or departments, as appropriate (e.g., CEO, Corp. Comms., HR, PR)	Postincident activities planned and executed
17.	Document findings, close ticket: Documentation should have been occurring throughout the process. At this time, verify that all documentation created by others has been collected and update it with any new findings and conclusions. Close the incident ticket.	Responders and investigators	All documentation complete and centralized Ticket closed
18.	Postmortem and remediation: Determine appropriate parties to be involved in the postmortem discussion. Schedule and conduct the postmortem meeting to review the incident and determine any procedural or technical changes needed to ensure that the incident does not recur or that the response next time will be faster. Oversee execution of remediation.	EIT	Meeting conducted with appropriate attendees Lessons learned documented Remediation plans executed

The Frontline

Detecting the Incident

Every incident begins with some form of detection. Detection can occur via calls to the help desk, log reviews, intrusion detection alerts, an anomalous event on the network or systems, etc. The frontline comprises individuals who are the eyes and ears of your organization. They typically initiate the incident response process because they are your detective mechanisms. Depending on your organization, you may compose your frontline differently. In the following list, we identify groups found in most companies and why they should be represented in the frontline:

- The security monitoring group scrutinizes security-related activity in your environment and may come across a security incident.
- The help desk could receive calls from the user population that are indicative of a security event.
- The network monitoring group scrutinizes activity on the network and may notice an anomalous event.
- The platform monitoring group scrutinizes activity on platforms and may notice an anomalous event.
- Desktop support services the user population and may come across a security-related incident.
- System administrators work on the platforms and may notice an anomalous file or configuration.
- E-mail administrators monitor e-mail activity and may notice an anomalous event.

Frontline Objectives

Identifying your frontline is important because, as part of your CSIRT planning, you need to provide adequate training to these groups so that they can fulfill their CSIRT function. You need to educate them on:

- Capturing information that may be volatile (information that changes and therefore must be captured immediately)
- Capturing basic information accurately to aid in the response effort
- Weeding out obvious false positives
- Triggering the IRT process

Maximizing the Frontline

Remember that most of the frontline teams do not work for the information security department. Leveraging other groups to fulfill a security function is cost effective but you must invest in training and tools. Providing the frontline with an easy-to-use guide on how to detect incidents and what to do will greatly maximize the effectiveness of this group. Table 13.2 provides a template for accomplishing this. Many incidents are first reported to the help desk by the user as "something is wrong with my computer." This table presents questions that the help desk representative can ask to assist in determining whether the user's problem may be related to a security incident.

Table 13.2   Frontline Questions

Stage	Comments	Question Set
Initial	If any of the answers are "yes" or "not sure," go to next stage; otherwise, proceed with normal trouble-shooting procedures.	**Is the incident virus-related?** Antivirus warned the user of a suspicious file or activity Attachment was launched resulting in unusual system behavior (missing files, cannot boot up, etc.) Unusual pop-up windows asking the user to click on something Unusually high system activity on the user's computer User accused of sending e-mails to many people in his or her e-mail address book **Does the incident involve unauthorized or unlawful activities?** Theft (include electronic, e-mail, customer data, etc.) Unauthorized access Impersonation or identity theft Copyright infringement Violation of privacy Vandalism (include defacing Web sites and unauthorized deletion or modification of files) **Are the disruptions to service or functionality caused by unusual or unexplainable events?** User feels as if someone has been tampering with his or her files or e-mails User noticed some unusual activity on his or her system User cannot do certain tasks that he or she was able to do before

Details	The goal is to get accurate information to pass on to information security, record all answers to the question set and go to the next stage.	Basic question set:
		  What is the incident? Describe the incident.
		Get the following information:
		  Hardware/OS/software involved
		  IP address of compromised system
		  Physical location of system
		  Current status of system
		  How was the incident detected?
		  When was the incident detected?
		  What has been done to the computer since the incident and by whom?
		  What is the current impact? Note the caller's assessment; also note your assessment of the situation.

Table 13.2 (Continued)   Frontline Questions

Stage	Comments	Question Set
Action and severity	Helps you determine what to do and how soon to do it. If you are unsure about how to respond to an incident, contact your manager or shift supervisor.	Virus-related incidents: For all virus-related events, contact the information security department If there is no response from members of the initial response team, contact the chief information security officer (CISO) Unauthorized or unlawful events: For all suspicious activities, contact CISO immediately If CISO does not respond, contact any member of the information security department Unusual or unexplainable events: Open a trouble ticket and assign to the information security department

It is very important that help desk representatives accurately identify incidents because early detection and reporting can help limit the damage of the overall incident. This table can also be effectively used by other members of the frontline group in identifying a potential security incident.

You should conduct periodic CSIRT drills to test the frontline members on how they would react to different incidents. Drills could be scheduled or unscheduled. Unscheduled drills should still be communicated to set the right expectations, but instead of giving a specific date and time, you provide a date range in which you will run the drill scenario.

Initial Response Team —The Primary Experts

Confirming the Security Incident

The IRT is the first expert unit at the scene of the incident. Think of the frontline as the 911 operator and the IRT as the paramedics or police officer. The IRT should comprise groups that can add value to the definitive confirmation of a security incident. You do not want to involve too many participants unnecessarily due to the potential sensitivity of the incident as well as the possibility of complicating the issue with superfluous input. For example, if you are dealing with a potential e-mail virus, you engage the e-mail administrators, as opposed to the system administrators, to help you determine whether you have a security incident.

Select liaisons from different IT groups to be members of the IRT as appropriate. In some organizations, there is a rotating duty pager system in which different IT administrators respond to the on-call page. You could leverage the person who is on call to be the IRT member. You staff every IRT group with a member of your department as the leader. Your security architects, engineers, specialists, and any other senior security staff should all participate in the IRT.

The following recommendation advises forming different IRT groups based on incident types:

- E-mail virus: liaisons from information security, e-mail, and network groups
- Desktop virus: liaisons from information security, desktop, and network groups
- Server virus: liaisons from information security, server, and network groups
- Network outage or service degradation events: liaisons from information security, server, network, and telecom groups
- Suspicious or unlawful events: liaisons from information security, and possibly legal, physical security, or an external investigations group

Objectives of the IRT

The goals of the IRT are:

- Determine quickly whether the incident is real or false and its severity (if real).
- Resolve the incident, if possible, or escalate accordingly.
- Obtain enough information to determine next steps.
- Apply sound forensics principles and alter the state of the system as little as possible for a hacking incident.
- Report back to the CISO immediately.

The frontline may notice an anomalous event but its members do not have the appropriate expertise to confirm a real event from a false positive definitively. The IRT's role is to investigate the reported incident and confirm or deny its validity. In your planning stage, you should have created an incident toolbox with various executables that can quickly identify security events. If you are dealing with a possible hacking activity, your toolbox should consist of a script that would obtain the following information quickly:

- Current processes and services running on the system
- Users who have logged onto the system for the past two weeks
- Current ports listening on the system and the corresponding application running the listener
- Executables that start up when the system reboots
- Key system files changed in the last two weeks

Most of the tools that can extract this information are available as freeware. If you have invested in an end-point security or a host-based intrusion detection solution, then build the appropriate procedures around your tools to get a definitive identification of the incident. If you are dealing with virus activity, your toolbox should consist of various monitoring capabilities that can help you pinpoint the source and spread of the virus and where the appropriate choke points may be. The key thing here is to have these tools identified before the event and have your IRT trained on using them appropriately.

After collecting all of the current system data and determining that an incident is in progress, the IRT tries to determine the severity of the event and whether to escalate the issue. In the event that the incident is resolvable, the IRT can take the appropriate measure to address a developing event before it becomes a full-scale security incident. For example, if a virus is just starting to propagate, the team can immediately pull the network cable and monitor to see whether there are any other infected machines to remedy.

In other instances, the IRT is engaged when the event has already affected a significant number of people. In those scenarios, the IRT needs to report back immediately to the CISO and let him or her engage the EIT to determine the appropriate next steps.

Initial Response Procedure

These steps should be followed to establish the procedure for the IRT:

1. IRT is notified of an incident by the frontline.
2. IRT gathers to verify the incident.
3. IRT collects volatile information on implicated systems if it is associated with hacker activity:
   System date and time
   A list of currently running processes

A list of currently open sockets or ports

The applications listening on open sockets or ports

A list of the users who are currently logged on

A list of the systems that have current or had recent connections to the system

4. IRT monitors network and system traffic closely if it is a virus activity.
5. IRT decides based on data collected whether the incident is real.
6. If the incident is real, IRT will contact the CISO.
7. While the CISO develops his or her plan of attack, the IRT members should continue with the following activities:

Capture any volatile information

Obtain the updated network diagram pertaining to the incident

Obtain the updated contact list of business managers who have decision-making authority surrounding the incident

Open an incident log to track the incident and post relevant information

Initiate increased monitoring activities on the network, system, and affected applications

Once again, this procedure is a model that you can tailor to suit the needs of your organization so that you can meet the goals of the IRT procedure: analyze, confirm, escalate, and contain.

Executive Incident Team —The Decision Makers

The impact of a security incident is far reaching and could severely affect the company's liability or ability to do business. Key decisions need to be made in short order to prevent further damage. For example, if you discover an active hacking event that is siphoning off confidential customer data, do you stop the activity and tip off the hacker or do you allow more data to be stolen while you track the attacker? The dilemma is that if you alert the hacker, you may never recover the material stolen so far, but if you do not stop the attack, more data is compromised. Another example is a virus incident that could corrupt data files and could spread to production systems. Do you take down your ability to do business temporarily to protect the integrity of your data? The point of these examples is to illustrate the importance of getting the right decision makers involved at a very early stage of a high-impact incident. The CISO cannot make these decisions alone due to the substantial repercussions of such decisions. The EIT is the forum for these difficult decisions.

The key to selecting your EIT members is to ask the question of whether they have relevance to resolving an incident, as well as the authority to make important decisions that could have a significant impact on the company. Our recommendation is to involve the following executives if possible:

- Chief information officer to activate technology solutions to address the incident
- Chief information security officer to provide security subject matter expertise and risk calculations in an incident
- Chief privacy officer to assess the privacy and regulatory implications of the incident
- Chief operating officer to represent the business interest during an incident
- General legal counsel to provide the legal perspective in an incident
- Vice president of Public Relations or Corporate Communications to consider the public relations aspect in an incident

Depending on your company's organizational composition and culture, you may opt to engage directors instead of senior executives. The idea is to get people that are authorized to make decisions in a crisis.

Objectives of the EIT

The responsibilities of the EIT in an incident include:

- Propose a response strategy or approve a proposed response strategy to best handle the incident based on the circumstances at hand.
- Designate the managers, associates, or third-party individuals who will be involved in resolving or investigating the incident.
- Manage communications about the incident from corporate and public relations perspectives
- Provide relevant reporting up to senior executive management (if the EIT is composed of lower level executives such as directors).
- Conduct a postmortem on an incident and initiate remediation or damage control activities.

Response Strategy

Every company has different sets of priorities and no two security incidents are completely alike. The EIT has the burden of choosing a response strategy that is aligned to the company's risk appetite while addressing the different nuances of the incident. Table 13.3 shows

Table 13.3   Response Priorities and Associated Activities

Response Priority	Description of Possible Activities
Protect data integrity and confidentiality	Take affected systems offline immediately to prevent further compromise of data Determine extent to which customer or sensitive corporate data has been compromised Consider legal implications around CSIRT process Employ objective third party to validate forensics activities Engage corporate communications and investor relations teams as needed
Publicity control	Expedite incident handling procedures with accountability as top priority Brief employees on appropriate dissemination of information Plan to manage public and media expectations
Resume operations	Perform recovery activity before containment or eradication activity Troubleshoot operations issues without taking system offline, if possible Make decision whether to invest less time and fewer resources gathering evidence Decide whether to accept risk of further contamination Perform containment and eradication activity during off-peak hours or maintenance windows, if possible
Cleanse site	Stop all possible avenues of contamination Consider taking system offline for thorough eradication and recovery process Harden system to prevent security relapse

Table 13.3 (Continued)   Response Priorities and Associated Activities

Response Priority	*Description of Possible Activities*
Prosecute intruder	Decide whether to allocate time and resources to build legal case against intruder (Note: The decision to prosecute can significantly affect the way an investigation is conducted. It is advisable to consult with your legal department and establish whether you will prosecute intruders as a corporate policy and under what circumstances. If the decision is that sometimes the company may wish to prosecute, each incident should initially be handled as if a prosecution will ensue, until a decision not to prosecute has been made.)
	Maintain status quo so as not to tip off intruder
	Accept and manage risk of allowing intruder to remain in system
	Involve professional security investigators early in process to collect evidence for forensics analysis
	Create decoy systems (honey pots) to better monitor intruder activities
	Involve legal and law enforcement departments

how different response priorities change the course of action for the CSIRT. After an incident occurs, the response will involve a number of activities that are prioritized in such a way as to keep the business going while minimizing damage. The priorities are listed in this table, along with a set of activities that need to occur for each priority.

In some cases, the EIT may decide to take hybrid approaches or switch gears depending on the outcome of a certain strategy. Once again, a scenario-based CSIRT drill is important in developing these decision-making skills.

Considering Prosecution

As part of the initial establishment of an incident response process, the EIT should be engaged in making a policy decision related to prosecution. It should be very clear to the CSIRT whether the company intends to prosecute intruders or simply stop them from doing damage. If there are conditions when one or the other is the correct course of action, the CSIRT should also understand what those conditions are. This is so important because if the company wishes to prosecute, there will be a lot more work involved on the part of the CSIRT in terms of gathering evidence, chain of custody, and documentation so that the corporate lawyers later have what they need in court.

If the company has a blanket stance that it will never prosecute, the CSIRT will be saved quite a bit of extra work. If the company has a blanket stance that it will always prosecute, the CSIRT must do the right things from the first moment; otherwise, the evidence may be compromised or inadequate and become inadmissible in court. If the company reserves the right to prosecute, the CSIRT must assume that each incident will be prosecuted and follow the path of collecting court-admissible evidence. This will continue until it is determined that no prosecution will occur for a particular incident or unless the CSIRT can determine definitively up front, based on clearly defined criteria, whether this particular incident is subject to prosecution or not.

EIT Procedure

The EIT will follow certain procedures when notified of an incident:

- Receive notification (phone call or page) from the CISO with meeting logistics and a quick briefing on the incident.
- Dial in to the CSIRT conference line or gather onsite to discuss the incident.
- Engage other key players as needed (CEO, CFO, subject matter experts, Investor Relations, etc.).
- Decide on course of action or response strategy based on limited facts.
- Designate responders to work on bringing the system back to operational status.
- Designate investigators to identify root cause and propose recommendations.
- Define short-term objectives.
- Establish checkpoint meetings to track the progress of the incident resolution.
- Make adjustments to response strategy based on the checkpoint meetings.

- Review and approve incident report.
- Report to senior management as appropriate.
- Initiate remediation or damage control plan.

Responders—The Recovery Experts

Responders are the people who get things back to normal. A large-scale security incident upsets the equilibrium of your business functions and calls for experts who can effectively devise a plan of attack to contain and stabilize the effects of the incident. Your responders are typically technical heavyweights in the various IT silos such as network, e-mail, systems, applications, etc. They know where to look to find clues about the incident's behavior and what to do in different scenarios. They can pull up appropriate monitoring tools, pore over cryptic logs, or get into consoles and make on-the-fly configuration changes that could stop the incident from causing more damage. These individuals must think fast on their feet and act fast with their hands once they get the mandate from the EIT to address the incident.

Objectives

The goals of the responders are:

- Assess the scope and damage of an incident and execute a containment and recovery plan.
- Control and contain the incident using proper escalation and collaboration processes.
- Establish communication lines to all relevant parties on a need-to-know basis.
- Capture relevant information for investigators.

Because responders are already experts in their fields, the CSIRT training for them is geared toward guiding them through the process. Scenario-based training and a healthy roundtable discussion to play out what they would do in different circumstances could be extremely beneficial.

Responders' Guidelines

As opposed to a set procedure, responders operate more in a guideline mode, depending on where the incident takes them. The following outlines recommended activities on which a responder should focus in an incident:

- If it is a virus-related incident, try to obtain a couple of infected systems and watch their mode of propagation in a "sandbox" environment.
- Step up monitoring and reconnaissance activities to collect all pertinent information.
- Control user access to affected systems and limit any other new variables entering the equation.
- Interpret logs or symptoms to identify the mode of attack.
- Do not reboot or change the system before capturing volatile information or verifying the possible implications of the reboot.
- Systematically follow leads until the cause of the failure, malfunction, or anomaly is isolated.
- Note any key breakthroughs or artifacts in the incident log to share with the investigators.
- Consult with the CISO or EIT before launching system changes to contain the incident.
- Contain the incident.
- Restore the affected systems to full functionality.
- Note action taken in the incident log.
- Synchronize data points about the incident with the investigators.

Investigators—The Root Cause Analysts

In any security incident, you have the burden of recovery as well as root cause analysis. You want to get your business systems back to operational mode, but you also need to know what vulnerability was exploited and where the incident started so that you can take steps to prevent a future occurrence. While your responders are moving at lightning pace to turn the lights back on, your investigators are the ones who carefully comb through logs and follow the scent of the incident to its source.

Objectives

The goals of the investigators are:

- Use an organized, formal investigative process to retain chain-of-custody and evidentiary integrity (if prosecution is a goal).
- Provide relevant information to responders.

- Act as liaisons to law enforcement and legal authorities and provide expert testimony (if prosecution is a goal).
- Provide management with recommendations on preventing future occurrences after conferring with the responders.

The investigative role is more involved in a hacking incident than a virus outbreak. In the case of a virus, the investigator will work with the responder to review the network or intrusion detection logs to find the origin of the infected machine, also called the zero-host. Once the zero-host is found, the investigator would examine the system to identify how the virus got in.

In a hacking incident, the investigator must put on his or her digital forensics hat and carefully approach the scene of the breach. Not every organization can afford to staff a forensics expert or procure court-approved forensics tools. A cost-effective way to manage this is to outsource the forensics activities to a certified professional that can provide expert services and testify in court if the need arises. Regardless of who does it, the investigator must carefully collect incriminating material so as to preserve evidentiary integrity. He or she must search and interpret cryptic logs to reconstruct the events leading up to the incident. The investigator must image or confiscate certain hardware for further examination or to protect the evidence. The extent to which the investigator works to preserve evidence is largely driven by the response priorities set by the EIT. If the EIT has a priority of prosecuting the intruder, then the evidence collection becomes crucial and must be done in a way that can be presented as viable proof in the court of law.

Investigators' Guidelines

The following recommended activities should be performed by an investigator:

- Stay in close communications with the responders.
- Execute or skip forensics imaging in accordance with the EIT's response strategy.
- Keep a written log of all investigative activities.
- Collect as much information as possible without changing the system.
- Use trusted binaries to execute commands on the system and pipe output to a secure forensics server or disk.

- Systematically investigate each lead and timestamp all investigative activities.
- Note any key breakthroughs or artifacts in the incident log to share with the responders.
- Collaborate with responders to identify root or probable cause along with recommendations.
- Prepare a root cause analysis and present it to the EIT.

Postmortem of an Incident

Once the dust settles and you have received the appropriate root cause analysis from the investigator, it is time to take a close look at preventative measures. Because the EIT has executive jurisdiction over the incident, it is appropriate to involve it in the decision-making process of the remediation or damage control effort.

An effective way to facilitate the postmortem discussion is to package all the relevant information into an executive incident summary. The summary should contain the following information:

- Key facts about the incident
- If it was a virus activity, the impact that it had on similar companies in your industry to draw a comparison of how effective your process was
- High-level time line of key turning points in the incident response activity
- Delineation of the business impact of the incident, including total downtime, number of people affected, key systems affected, and, if possible, a cost estimate for the damage
- Delineation of the effort required to address the incident, including total number of people mobilized and using an average hourly rate to estimate the total cost of recovery
- The root cause analysis and vulnerability exploited
- Remediation or damage control recommendations and action items, for different alternatives, including pros and cons

Once you have the executive incident summary completed, call your postmortem meeting with the EIT and discuss next steps. The summary is also a great tool for the EIT to communicate the incident to peers or relevant parties.

Another postmortem activity that is often overlooked is to do an analysis on your CSIRT process. There are probably lessons to be gleaned from every execution of the CSIRT process and these improvements should be included in the next revision of your incident handling methodology. This ensures that your CSIRT is, and continues to be, as efficient and effective as possible.

Recap of the Incident Response Process

Table 13.4 provides an at-a-glance summary of the CSIRT process discussed in this chapter.

Table 13.4 Phases of Response Process, Including Description of Each Response and Associated Activities

Phases	Description	Activities
Preincident preparation	Take action to prepare before an incident happens	Establish objectives for CSIRT Identify CSIRT members and establish roles and responsibilities Establish clear communication, escalation, response, and reporting protocols Prepare, equip, and train frontline teams to be first line of response Establish processes for EIT to arrive at a response decision Prepare, equip, and train CSIRT to handle and resolve incidents Raise awareness with Information Security Steering Committee (ISSC) and executive board Conduct CSIRT drills and training
Detection of incidents	Obtain enough information to determine whether incident is security related; if so, notify initial response team	Establish alert procedures to enable frontline teams to capture accurate information, assign severity level, and contact IRT Establish triggers in network, system, and application monitoring tools to automatically send alerts Establish event tracking mechanism and start an incident log

(continued)

Table 13.4 (Continued)   Phases of Response Process, Including Description of Each Response and Associated Activities

Phases	Description	Activities
Initial response	Obtain enough information to determine appropriate response	Identify initial response team IRT members Establish IRT procedures to classify incident quickly and respond accordingly Capture volatile evidence before it is lost Apply sound forensics principles and alter state of system as little as possible Obtain enough information to determine next steps Train IRT to escalate appropriately to EIT
Step up monitoring	Increase monitoring activities to investigate and secure the system	Increase monitoring activities from initial response to recovery phases of incident Establish central point of contact, collection, and reporting of CSIRT monitoring activities
Response strategy formulation	EIT reviews facts, determines best response, and obtains appropriate approvals	Establish process to get accurate information to EIT meeting Establish response protocol: make CSIRT conference bridge line available or conduct face-to-face meeting at designated conference room or site Provide guidelines for analysis, decision making, and escalation protocols to arrive at response strategy Response strategy determines details and extent of forensics, investigation, secure measure implementations, monitoring and recovery strategies
Forensics	Execute forensics activities and maintain appropriate evidentiary integrity	Engage a forensics expert to gather evidence with integrity Establish chain-of-custody and evidence-handling procedures

Table 13.4 (Continued)   Phases of Response Process, Including Description of Each Response and Associated Activities

Phases	Description	Activities
Investigation and verification	Detailed root cause analysis; involve objective third party; this runs parallel with containment activities	Assign investigator to case to conduct root cause analysis Consider involving objective third-party security firm to collaborate with CSIRT Establish investigation protocols to interview personnel, run analysis tools, capture pre-existing configurations, gather and review logs
Contain and isolate	Isolate and contain incident to enable business continuity; this is a parallel effort with investigative activities	Implement control measures as outlined by response strategy Isolate and contain infected or compromised systems from affecting the business
Recovery	Restore the system to operational state	Contingent on completion of containment activities and input from investigative phase Compromised or infected systems must be sanitized and secured before reinstatement
Postmortem activities	Activities are conducted after the incident to provide an accounting of the incident to executive management, establish risk mitigation initiatives to address weaknesses, and improve the CSIRT process	Establish reporting procedures to preserve and disseminate information regarding incident accurately and securely Address legal, HR, PR implications Notify internal audit and executive management as appropriate Provide recommendations to mitigate risks Establish verification process for validating security controls put in place to mitigate identified risk area Establish process for capturing improvements to CSIRT process

Index

Milton Keynes UK
Ingram Content Group UK Ltd.
UKHW040109071024
449327UK00019B/940